Only In Love
Poems

Only In Love
Poems

Phani Mohanty

Translated by
Dr. Sonali Sahu

BLACK EAGLE BOOKS
Dublin, USA | Bhubaneswar, India

Black Eagle Books
USA address:
7464 Wisdom Lane
Dublin, OH 43016

India address:
E/312, Trident Galaxy, Kalinga Nagar,
Bhubaneswar-751003, Odisha, India

E-mail: info@blackeaglebooks.org
Website: www.blackeaglebooks.org

First International Edition Published by
Black Eagle Books, 2025

ONLY IN LOVE (Poems)
by Dr. Phani Mohanty
Translated by **Dr. Sonali Sahu**

Original Copyright © Dr. Phani Mohanty
Translation Copyright © Dr. Sonali Sahu

All rights reserved. No part of this publication may be reproduced, stored in a retrieval system, or transmitted, in any form or by any means, electronic, mechanical, photocopying, recording or otherwise without the prior permission of the publisher.

Cover & Interior Design: Ezy's Publication

ISBN- 978-1-64560-759-5 (Paperback)

Printed in the United States of America

*I dedicate this book to the Supreme Power —
Radhakrishna, the divine epitome of
eternal love and spiritual harmony.*

Preface

The palpable transformations across the global arena in the aftermath of the cyber revolution and information technology explosion caused serious concern among aficionados of literature about its future. But their apprehensions appeared to be unfounded when literature withstood the onslaughts and emerged unruffled, being ensconced on a firm saddle. Literature, with its diverse genres, entertains and enlightens readers with new insights and perspectives on life, releasing them from the labyrinth of cares and anxieties, and infusing in them resilience and enthusiasm.

A creative writer observes the situations with his organic sensibility and shares his emotions and feelings passionately through objective correlatives. The writer, by the alembic of his imagination, creates an oasis in the desert of life, paints a rainbow amid the stormy tumult of society. The writer's alchemy of creativity with the wizardry of images enthrals the readers, keeping them in a mesmerizing spell.

Against this backdrop, it is seen that translation occupies a paramount position in promoting literature on an international platform with a wider clientele. The poetry collection in Odia, "Kebala Premare" of the renowned Neo Romantic poet Dr Phani Mohanty, is translated into English as "Only in Love" by Dr Sonali Sahu. Dr Sahu has done a wonderful job in making an impeccable transfer of feelings, emotions, and thoughts of the veteran poet Dr Mohanty from the source language to the target language. I am sure she must have come across problems in finding substitutes for certain emotions, colloquial expressions, yet she has managed to overcome them by presenting the tone, tenor, and essence of feelings. Poetry in Indian languages contains certain features, such as verbal imageries, local myths, inflections, and colloquialisms, that prove to be a translator's nightmare. Dr Sahu, with her maturity, expertise, and command over both languages, has successfully overcome the situation.

The veteran poet Dr Mohanty meticulously adheres to the poetic diction suggested by Wordsworth, always using ordinary, common, simple, and colloquial language really used by men in their day-to-day lives, for which he is widely hailed by the readers as a Neo-Romantic poet. Dr Mohanty's poetic career spanning across five decades with more than six dozen poetry collections, numerous awards and accolades like Odisha Sahitya Akademi and Kendriya Sahitya Akademi have endeared him to the charmed circle of hordes of readers for his unique theme of love, longing, regret, passion, despair, and positive affirmation depicted with simple diction, colloquial language, and lucid expression flowing uninterruptedly from a weary heart stirred with the subtle nuances and vagaries of love.

In this Collection of poems, "Only in Love," Dr Mohanty treats the concept of love as a pilgrimage of the human soul, an endless journey from the known to the unknown, from the physical to the metaphysical, from the real to the surreal, from the terrestrial to the ethereal, from the amorous to the philosophical and from the trivial to the sublime dimensions. The emotions, feelings, and passions in colloquial idioms unwaveringly flow like a stream where the heart understands perfectly, long before the mind attempts to decode it.

Dr Mohanty's poetic oeuvre builds up feelings of silence, speaking volumes of longing, inability, pining, shortcomings, and unfulfilled desires, that are carefully shaped into philosophical insights. Each poem in this collection is a glowing lamp illuminating the lanes of desire, loss, wonder, serenity, and redemption with a loud message that love understands those who patiently wait with warm, guileless hearts. Here, love is not limited to the boundary of the meeting between two lovers; rather, it is a metaphysical force binding the ecstasy of hope with the ache of memory, the thrill of union with the calm of surrender. The poems warmly invite the readers to navigate leisurely, listen intently, and feel deeply as to how the lines remind them that love, with all its uncertainty, fragility, mystery, and infinite dimension, is the most profound philosophy of human life.

I would like to take this opportunity to congratulate the Poet and the Translator for their exemplary devotion and unwavering commitment to present this wonderful Poetry Collection to the readers on a Global platform and enrich the repertoire of world literature. I wish the Poetry Collection in Translation "Only in Love" great success.

Kamala Prasad Mahapatra

Translator's Note

Dr. Phani Mohanty is widely recognized as a modern Neo-Romantic poet, deeply rooted in the Odia language, literature, and culture. His mastery of Odia vocabulary, colloquialisms, and the nuances of everyday speech allows him to connect effortlessly with both urban and rural audiences. The lucidity of his poetic language, his inventive use of ornamental words, and his remarkable ability to avoid overindulgence in metaphors, similes, and symbols make his poetry highly communicative, accessible, and deeply resonant for readers across diverse backgrounds. For these qualities, his poetry is widely enjoyed and celebrated. Dr. Mohanty has received numerous awards, including the prestigious Sahitya Akademi Award, and is rightly regarded as one of India's eminent poets. Some of his mythic and legendary works—such as Ahalya, Vishadyoga, Priyataman, Rutambara, and Maheswari—are profound, mind-boggling, and exemplary in both imagination and craft.

Translating Only in Love (Kebala Premare) into English has been a journey of reverence, surrender, and discovery. His exploration of love—the ecstasy of union, the ache of separation, and the sacred intimacy of desire—resonates as both universal and uniquely Odia. To bring these verses across languages demanded more than word-for-word fidelity; it required an immersion into rhythm, silence, breath, and the emotional undercurrent of each image.

Often, while translating, I found myself dwelling inside the poems, as if I too were walking through his landscapes of longing. When I rendered lines like—
"What is day, what is night—
as though seven thousand dawns and dusks
have pressed their weight upon the hours"
—I felt the crushing vastness of time in love's absence. And when I carried across his image of the restless self—
"The river of dreams leaps across its banks,
flowing in dazzling, thundering dance.
And I—like a leaf adrift,
floating in floodwaters,
belong neither here
nor there."
—I too became a part of that existential drift, where longing is both burden and liberation.

Each poem held me captive in its music—at times whispering tenderly, at times echoing with unbearable ache. Lines such as—
"Like an ancient document,
half seen, half erased,
bearing the faded mark
of a broken signature"
—reminded me of how love inscribes itself into memory, both luminous and fragile.

There were moments during translation when I felt overwhelmed by the intimacy of his voice. The words seemed to breathe on the page, carrying with them not just emotions but lived experience. To hold those delicate shades of passion in another language was like carrying water in cupped hands—always aware of how easily its essence might slip away. Yet, in that vulnerability, I discovered the beauty of translation itself: it is not about perfection, but about resonance.

I also realized how these poems mirror our own fragile journeys of love and loss. As I translated, I was not merely rendering Odia into English—I was also listening to the echoes of my own heart. This book is therefore not only a window into Dr. Mohanty's vision but also a mirror in which readers may see themselves reflected. In that sense, Only in Love is not just a collection of poems—it is an invitation to inhabit love in its many forms, and to recognize how it transforms us, even in silence, even in absence.

This work has not merely been a task of translation but an act of devotion. In the process, I have discovered not only the universality of Dr. Mohanty's romantic vision but also the intimate Odia essence that makes it extraordinary. My deepest hope is that this anthology will allow poetry lovers across the world to enter his luminous world of passion, vulnerability, and transcendence—to feel, as I have felt, the pulse of love that lingers in every verse.

Through this rendering, his voice, his vision, and his heart transcend the boundaries of language, inviting readers to dwell in the eternal realm of love he so masterfully creates.

Dr. Sonali Sahu

Contents

Ahalya
Two blue eyes
Understanding
Longing
Vain Attempt
Rutambara
The Hour Has Come
Take From Me Whatever You Desire
Painted Idol
The Mansoon Is Coming
The Illusion of Distance
Where are you
Not Now
Song of Love
The Lone Woman of a Barren Earth.
Sometimes
The Time of Departure
What Feelings Stir
Who Will Mend The Heart
Since you left
Jealousy
Vision within Vision
Close Enough to Feel
Riverbank
Hermitage
Will You Go Once ?
Enchantress
In A Crowd
One Day At Night
Today, She Arrives
Who Are You ?
Devil

Devil (1)
Devil (2)
Once Again, My Beloved
Begger Woman
Bisakha
Beloved
The Season And It's Absence
In Thirteen Days
Madness
In This Midnight Hour
While Leaving Home
The Passionate Lover
The Sacred Boundary
Will Go, But !
The Hope Of Baitarani
When Will You Return
Memory
Canvas
Meloncholy
Set No Terms
Devi
Solitary in the Emerald Woods
Alaka Sanyal
Your Graceful Body
Body
The First Evidence
Sheltered In Safety
After So Many Years
Termite Beneath The Tree
Queen
Love
My Beloved
Devi
Enraptured by Her Love

Ahalya

From whose tender, silken touch
did my sleep suddenly break,
Into the leaves, the flowers,
Onto the wood of the death bed,
The funeral pyre,
Into the floating clouds,
In the cascading streams of rain —
A ceaseless rain of divine sweetness
Began to flow.

Oh my soulmate across lifetimes!
Come to me —
As a sweet, sweet fragrance,
As a soft, melodious song.
Envelop me,
Stir my spirit,
Make me tremble with joy,
Enrapture me, enchant me —
In the divine downpour of celestial bliss.

After churning the skies,
Come forth in radiant light—
Riding a chariot of clear skies.
To this abandoned, hollow courtyard,
Come as a clay garland of five-colored flowers.

To the desolate island of night
Adorned with scattered stars,
Come—
As the pure, lotus-hearted bloom
Of love and compassion,
To my worn, rejected palace
Of a life unclaimed.

Upon your soft feet, hued in crimson dawn,
Tinkles the anklet — bejeweled with delicate diamonds.
In the ballad of a broken jasmine's longing,
Echoes the deep music of eternal sorrow.
On the trembling wings of a torn cloud,
Flows the silvery veil of forgiveness and grace.
O eternal companion of my dreams!
In both realms — the earthly and the ethereal —
In every moment, in every breath,
The melody of your gentle voice
Keeps resonating through my soul.

In the resounding downpour of monsoon rains,
On a deep Krishna-hued chariot,
In the dew-kissed, clear and tender dawn,
Through the dense, fragrant groves of longing and union,
In the soft, mad breeze of the southern wind —
Float toward me.
Touch me.
Embrace and sanctify this body, this courtyard,
Every atom of my blissful being,
Every spark of my awakened soul.

Enthrall me in the rhythm of Vedic chants,
And soothe my restless, storm-tossed spirit.

The dusky dust of dense clouds in your flowing hair,
And sluggish streams of rain cascading down…
In the evening sky, hues of crimson flare,
Where silver stars shimmer, softly crowned.
Within the forest of unspoken desires,
By the blue sea of tainted pride,
Each limb breathes a breeze of fragrance,
Each note — a restless song inside.

Far away, in a realm of half-shadow, half-light,
You dwell —
Like a flute of dusky love,
Unaware of its own longing.
Slowly, in the moonlight,
Within the music,
It weaves a melody —
Echoing in the fearless silence
Of your speechless presence.
And in that resonance,
My entire being burns —
Enfolded in the tender drape
Of your soft, celestial love.
Across the vast sky,
In dream and memory alike,
You spread —
O dark-hued charioteer of night,
O Eighth Rudra, O inviolable destiny —
In your glory,
Today, I am glorified.

Two blue eyes

How many unspoken tales brim in your eyes—
Eyes tinted with the serene blue
A sea of unsaid words
rests quietly on your silken lashes.
Just a fistful of borrowed time,
and with it, life itself slips away…

In the dark wine of your eyes,
My essence fades,
Drenched in ecstasy, lost in surrender.
I reel—intoxicated, consumed,
By the storm of your burning gaze.
Like a wounded bull in its final charge,
I glimpse the ancient script of my soul—
Scorched, shattered, undone.

In the womb of the primal sky,
The eagle of love flutters its wings—restless, wild.
In the thick hush of a wordless night,
Your closed eyes bloom open on their own.
Just before the deep, black silence
of this untamed dusk
fades into nothingness.
Your eyes cradle endless tales,
Yet you still choose to speak.

And when you don't—
Ah, how eloquently your silence
unfolds a universe of words.

Sometimes, you become silence itself—
Like a meditative sage, deep in trance.
And then, without warning,
You flow like a fearless river,
Unbridled, eloquent, unstoppable.

On the lush, surrendered bed of Sawan's rain,
You sleep beneath a languid, silver moon,
Weaving an unheard melody—so rare, so raw.
In every nerve, every breath,
Within the nirvana of sacred union,
You carve trembling figures of blood and flesh.
You gather the wandering crowd of aching stories,
And with each deep breath,
You fill soul and body with the weight of the five elements.
Then—drenched in dense, sacred embrace—
Place a kiss,
and let all creation dissolve into us.

Your eyes are brimming with untold stories—
Stories, in those two blue eyes of yours.
An ocean of unspoken words,
Resting quietly on the lashes
of your twin eyes.
And in their gentle blink,
A handful of life slips away—
And with it, the journey called existence ends.

Understanding

A city—eternally known,
etched into the folds of memory.
Where you exist.
Where I do, too.
Three decades have passed like a hush,
yet we never quite find each other.
Wearing garments of absence,
we drift—
like unsatisfied spirits
caught in the tangled branches of the wind.

Words spin like fire—
restless, wild—
a circle ablaze with no direction,
like a storm that forgot its destination,
like a maddened tornado
roaring
through a blazing sun
on a road that leads to nothing.

Familiar—achingly so—
is the city that holds us both.
We lived there, remember?
Year after year,
like silent stars

unseen by the world.
In a nameless gust, reckless and fierce,
the wind murmurs syllables
no one remembers.
It flows through a star
that may never have been.

And in that star,
your quiet pride,
your unspoken longing,
flickers—
like the uncertain flame of a lamp
fighting the wind,
burning in a moonlight
that forgets to glow.

Longing

You are the hushed horizon's endless sky,
The embodied season of longing embrace.
Love of the heavens, eternal and high,
A fiery shadow in a garden's grace.

You are the silver moon of the blue sky,
A star untouched by earthly desire.
The tender key to dream's soft bed,
The flowing stream of love and care.

In the lazy moon of desireless dawn,
Softly, slowly, the song of love is born.
In the firecrackers of passion's flame,
This earth burns, again and again.

When you are near, the night overflows
With honeyed fragrance, sweet and deep.
When you are gone, the earth feels hollow,
A tuneless silence, empty in grief.

Beloved, come with motherly grace,
Hand in hand, let us entwine.
With jasmine woven through your hair,
In the bower we'll weave a new delight.

Vain Attempt

I long for such a woman,
Whose crimson-tinted feet
Adorned with golden anklets,
Will tinkle sweetly in the gentle breeze

I long for such a woman,
In whose tender body of youth
Desires will blossom like flowers on trees,
And fall, trembling, in the forest wild.

I long for such a woman,
Whose voice and rhythm awaken
The melody of Raga Malhar
Rising through the groves of tamal trees.

In the grey dust of a womanless earth,
A poet's life writhes like a dying fish.
Amid vast palaces, in the fire of death,
The tender, sweet touch of a woman
Is like the nectar of immortality.
Every poet needs such a woman,
Who in the four corners of his consciousness
Touches each moment like blue poison,
Till every particle of his earthen body
Is absorbed into her like a deep blue shadow."
In this life, one longs
For such a woman's presence.

Rutambara

Amid the dwellings of unbearable sorrow,
My broken sleep drifts to the ten horizons.
Darkness chokes like mountains of ice,
Carved with the teeth of endless pain.
In courtyards of thick and thunderous cloud,
Lightning writhes like a suffocated fish.
The sky wears a garland of silence,
And every breath is heavy with longing's wound.

Her sari slipped, her loosened braid untamed,
In hues of blue and crimson she drifts,
Floating with the southern breeze.
The flute of Shyam sings,
While Shyam himself trembles in sudden disarray.
Then the innocent life, caught in tangled desire,
Beholds your unparalleled beauty,
And in rapture, my soul overflows.

In union, she is the wisdom of Prajñāpāramitā,
A glimpse of the woman's unearthly light.
She is the companion of enlightment
The exalted call of a soul's awakening.

She is the woman within womanless earth,
The goddess, the fierce Bhairavī,

The vast and immovable feminine,
The mysterious one, the all-destroying Earth.

She is the seed-sound of creation,
The first and final syllable of existence,
The resonance of dissolution's dance.
She is the mantra, the mandala, the mudra,
The woman who is love, compassion, and care—
The eternal, all-embracing feminine.

Her beauty is an enchantment divine,
On her feet, anklets of love sing cham-cham in rhythm.
Her body is no less than Vrindavan itself,
Where the weary soul finds its rest and renewal.

In the gentle breath of this breeze,
Her presence pervades all—
As if, within the secret bowers,
Every illusion is destroyed,
And only love remains.

Each syllable is steeped in beauty,
Each sound a drop of sweetest love.
Upon a couch of karanja blooms you rest,
Your body anointed with the fragrance of sandalwood.

O matchless maiden, robed in the season's grace,
Again and again, in Shyam's embrace,
This enchanted breeze goes wandering by—
Heavy with sighs of wonder,
And whispers of eternal love.

The Hour Has Come

The hour has come—
The hour to part from you,
To leave behind a final kiss,
Lingering like a fading flame upon your lips.

The hour has come—
To break the fragile chains of illusion,
To drift, like a homeless bird,
Into April's merciless silence,
And vanish softly,
Like a whisper erased from the sky.

The time has come—
To walk once more into
The sandalwood groves of the heart,
Where long ago I planted
The seed of memory.

The time has come—
To cast it into the fire of silence,
To let it perish in its own stillness.
In nameless, voiceless hours,
Without a word to anyone,
To dissolve, suddenly,
Like a cloud of illusion
Disappearing into the unseen.

As I bid you farewell,
You come before me
Like the radiant birds of dawn—
Your gaze, a melody without words,
Your breath, a song that stirs my soul.

Though your notes are nameless,
They burn within my heart—
Not as sorrow,
But as the fire of love
That refuses to fade.

Our love—
Like falling drops, fresh as tears,
A stream of sorrow and sweetness,
Most alluring in this mortal world.

In an unimaginable city of love,
I find myself transformed,
A reckless, wandering lover,
Lost in the fever of desire.

In the mischievous, fire-laden air,
I drift, restless—
From flower to flower,
From earth to sky,
And from one sky into another dreamscape.

Chasing visions upon visions,
Until at last, demanding from you
A final kiss—

I found you turned to stone,
A lifeless body in my arms.

Now the time has come
To bid you farewell—
With a smile upon my lips.

Take From Me Whatever You Desire

Take from me whatever you desire,
Ask for nothing, set no terms.

Draw from the veins of envy,
Bottle the blue fire of my blood.

And in that stream of sacrifice,
Let your loosened tresses bathe—
A dark forest of silken strands,
Consecrated in my crimson gift.

In the storm, I was bent and broken,
My blue flesh torn like the deceit of Indra.
Take my severed body away—
Feast upon it in your joy,
Make a festival of my pain.

Like Dadhichi's ancient, time-worn bones,
Shape gleaming weapons from each joint,
To strike against the terror,
To pierce the very heart of ruin.

faithful, evocative From my
whispering breath and your tender flute,

Let the raga swell and flood the hollow caves.
Let my trembling skeleton become your incense —
Set it ablaze, a lamp of vengeance in marrow and joy.
In defeat let the conch of victory be sounded;
Take what must be taken — keep no terms, set no bounds.

In my soaring pride, radiant as flame,
In your graceful stride of mystery, let me fall—
Break me gently into the beauty of your spell.
On the unseen stage of trust and soul,
Let me be lost in the rapture of your dance,
My remaining years entwined in the rhythm of your steps.
Take from me whatever you desire—
No bargains, no bounds, only love's surrender.

Upon the barren tree of Time,
like a lifeless bird I hang—
caught in the stillness of an unbearable hour.
A householder and yet a monk unborn,
I drift between being and unbeing,
between the echo and its silence.
Take from me what you will,
lay no bargain, bind me with no condition.

Painted Idol

Who is that eternal artist
who lights the canvas of stars,
draping the ancient sky
in unfading strokes of wonder?

From what forgotten aeon
did you vanish—
only to live on
in some immortal realm of silence,
where no messenger can reach,
no path bears your name,
and no dwelling holds your trace.

Where are you, O heart-enchanting one?
In which kingdom of senses do you dwell?

In the garlands of radiant lamps, or perhaps—
in the shimmering blue,
a jeweled cascade of light without a name.

In the boundless silence of the still sky,
you drift—
a broken cloud afloat,
or in the diamond-city of the great void,
wrapped in its smoky glow.

Where are you, O heart-stealing one—where?
Are you hidden in the trembling thunderclouds,
humming with the night's soft fragrance,
or scattered in the wounded strings of a guitar,
where a shattered raga
bleeds its aching music into the dark?
In the purest clarity
of infinite beauty's sweetness—
not in the homeward flight of birds,
chirping in reunion,
nor in the lazy rain
of an ancient August afternoon.

Where are you, O elusive one—
where?

Where are you, O soul-enchanting one?
Through all the years of living,
through all the hours of dying,
your song resounds—
a melody woven into the blue of endless skies.

Fresh blossoms of silver stars unfold,
while memory and forgetting alike
glimmer and fade
in the flickering lamps of dusk.

The Mansoon Is Coming

For whom have you stained your hands and feet
with the deep crimson of henna's breath?
For whom do you raise these fragile palaces of dreams,
even in the furnace of a burning noon?

Your eyes darkened with kohl,
your forehead aglow with sindoor—
tell me, for which astonished guest of destiny
have you kept vigil through the night,
feeding the lamp with your sleepless flame?

Through the night, a procession of light—
yet only darkness,
endless, unyielding darkness.

It sits sprawling,
like a devil nesting in the banyan's arms,
stretching its shadowed limbs.

In the futility of false promises,
like a witless bird
it circles the void,
spinning and spinning—
beneath the moon's pale fire,
within the vast blue silence of the sky.

In the lamp of memory,
the time of full blossom arrives.

On the silent lips of the sky,
a ghazal of clouds is written.

In the detached forest,
the night drifts intoxicated—
its lazy rhythm echoing softly,
while the tender moon of drizzling rain
yearns in restless melody,
calling—come, come!

Come in the radiance of the moon,
come to me,
O my beloved.

For whom have you graced your hands and feet
with the tender green of henna's bloom?
For whom have you kept the vigil of night,
guarding the flame of a faithful lamp?

The whispers are everywhere:
"He is coming, He is near!"
And the forest sways in song—
for Shyam, our eternal beloved,
is on his way.

The Illusion of Distance

When you are near,
my heart feels as if
the world itself is complete in my hands—
bliss, union, and rapture.
Yet my yearning cry
rings out,
trembling at the edge of fulfillment.

When you are not near,
nothing exists anywhere—
like spring without its fragrance,
or dark clouds that hold no rain.

Like the ocean's churn with neither poison nor nectar,
like the sky bereft of moon and sun,
like lightning without its flash,
like a canvas without its painting,
like a soul devoid of life's spark—

Nothing at all exists,
when you are not near.

I am drowning alone
in the vast ocean of myself.
What song could I sing

when my heart is empty,
and all around lies a hollow expanse?

In this gray, endless desert,
every melody falters,
every note is broken,
all because you are not here.

You are truly infinite,
perfect in every possibility—
a golden chalice,
a sacred spring leaping from Gangotri,
a dreamlike court of both desire and repentance.

A radiant manuscript of unforgotten memory,
you are the shimmering, earthen temple
of endless, unfolding potential.

For whom have you painted your hands and feet
with the fragrant green of henna's bloom?
For whom have you traced Radha–Krishna rangoli,
spreading across the flowering threshold,
like vines woven with color and devotion?

Amid the trembling glow of lamps,
you sit adorned in your spellbound beauty—
a living enchantment,
the very embodiment of longing's dream.

That darkness—
sprawled like a devil,

hands and feet stretched wide
in an unguarded hour—

on the weary currents
of time's desolate river,
where the innocent bird
of empty promises
circles and circles,
trapped in the faint glow
of false light.

For whom, then,
do you sit in your bewitching form,
waiting endlessly
in the twilight's long,
haunting silence?

Where are you

In the lamps of stars,
some eternal painter has adorned
the ancient sky with secret strokes.

At the signal of the unseen,
you vanished—
from some forgotten aeon,
into a realm beyond,
where no trace of you remains,
no echo of voice,
no whisper of song.

Where are you?

Are you hidden
in some kingdom of senses unknown,
in an undiscovered heaven,
a middle sky between worlds?

Where are you?
Where are you?

Not in the radiant garlands of lamps,
nor in the shimmering golden hues
of the endless blue sky.

Not in the vast, accursed silence
of the still and unfeeling heavens,
nor drifting like cotton-cloud chains
across their vacant expanse.

Not even in the great diamond-city
of the immense void—
you are nowhere to be found.
Where are you,
O soul-enchanting one,
cloaked in the garment
of the unseen?

In the humming thunderclouds of night,
within their electrified song,
in the fractured raga
bleeding from a guitar's strings,

in the birds returning home,
their chirping laced with tender longing,
yet not in the infinite sweetness
of soft tears unshed—

Where are you?

Where are you, O soul-enchanting one,
where are you?

Without you, everything here is half—
water half-drunk,
the betel leaf half-chewed,
nirvana incomplete,

bondage unfinished,
union unfulfilled,
even renunciation left unfinished.

You are, in truth,
the gentle, tender note
of a sweet and simple song.

You are, in truth,
the radiant signature
of an unforgettable memory.

Not Now

Not now—
but someday, we shall meet again,
as though seeing and not seeing,
as though meeting in a dream.

On a night soaked in rain,
drenched with the adornments of love,
in the languid passage of time.

Amid the flickering stars,
an endless tryst will unfold
in the moonlit corridors
of sky and shadow.

Clad in a sari of lunar glow,
you will come—
in the painted chariot of dusk,
your breath scented
with the intoxication of tender fragrance,
your hair adorned
with garlands of green jasmine.

You will come—
like the unbidden,

like sudden radiance
in the heart of darkness.

In your eyes
dawn breaks a hundred thousand times,
each sunrise a poem.

In your breath
flows the breeze,
scented with the sweetness of honey.

In your weary feet
runs the river of new seasons;
on your golden brow
shimmers the blue sky's glimmering light.

In your striving,
in your wisdom,
in your every journey—
there burns a secret fire of longing.

In the restless, trembling notes
of the flute's song,
in the homecoming cry
of the bird at dusk—

Love inscribes
its alluring signature,
in strokes of deepest blue.

You are, in every forest,
the serene sweetness of dawn;

in Gopalpur's salty air,
the stillness of the sky.

You are the lazy rhythm
of selfless love,
the honey-laden breeze
of a night of union,
drunk with desire.

Not now—
but someday, we shall meet again,
as though seeing,
as though not seeing.

In a rain-soaked night
laden with adornments of love,
in the charged and trembling hour,
in another world,
in the radiance of another sky.

Song of Love

Beloved, my love, today I must come—
I must come!
Casting aside every ritual,
Leaping across the lines of fate,
Spinning lies before master and mother-in-law,
Weaving falsehoods for the sisters-in-law too,
Cheating the household of its guard,
I arrive—
Alone, all alone,
Through the thick, unyielding forest—
Only to you.

Yet—there is no echo of his voice,
No fragrance of his body carried on the winds.
After the rustle of fallen leaves,
No silver-chime of the Lord's anklets reaches my ear.

Amid the tangle of vines,
No yearning flute-song trembles through the air.
In this vast orbit of being,
Your presence or absence bears no mark.

On the blue waters of Yamuna,
No crescent of light adorns the rising stream.
And within this body—

Is there life, or is there none?
I no longer have the strength to know.

Was it some unseen storm
that struck him on the road back?
How faithless he proves to be—
to let the promise of his coming
rise like a tide,
only to let it break
into the dust of silence.

To leave words unspoken—
that has become his chosen habit.
And here I sit,
the remnants of my life
burning desperately
for a single syllable from him.

The lovely garden around me
lies hollow and desolate,
its silence heavy,
its beauty drowned
in sorrow and despair.

The dusky shadow
of his dark, resplendent body
falls upon the barren afternoon—
scolding me,
like a lone scarecrow in the fields.

And beneath the moonlit sky,
no pathways appear,

no crossings can be seen—
only a bewildering void,
where his presence should have been.
Uncertain is your coming — uncertain your not coming;
After knowing this, what remains for me to do?
I simply sit — and sit —
my days folded into the plain, patient shape of waiting.

The Lone Woman of a Barren Earth.

Across the boundless earth,
where might such a woman be found—
whose white, conch-like veil
harbors the tender breeze of love and mercy,
fluttering its wings in quiet grace?

Within the crimson valleys of her eyes
a constellation-sown night reclines,
sinking into deep repose,
as though the stars themselves slumbered
upon a jeweled couch of dreams.

Where, on this wide and untamed earth,
might one find such a woman?
She who, like a fragment of the river of sorrow,
laughing, plucks flowers from blossoming trees.

Adorned with beautiful, delicate wings,
silver anklets chiming with every step,
her sound like gentle raindrops falling.

From the hidden chambers of Gandharva tunes
and the lonely flute's tender notes,
she drifts through dusk and dawn,
floating softly in the fullness of the rains.

Where on earth
might one find such a woman—
whose very body exhales fragrance
that stirs the winds even in the darkest days?
Leaping, again and again,
across borders and far-flung boundaries,
she blooms open
like a flower under the sun.

Gently, in the fall of leaves,
with hands raised in the blessing mudra,
upon the tranquil lawns of deep green,
amid the cool shadows,
the murmuring stream
will whisper its tinkling song.

In the shimmer of new possibilities,
in the silent morning,
her garments unfold like Draupadi's robes—
layer upon layer,
revealing themselves slowly,
softly,
with quiet grandeur.

Where on this vast, untamed earth
might one find such a woman—
so rare, so unparalleled?

Sometimes

(1)

Was it truly so urgent,
to arrive in such an inauspicious hour?
To slip in silently,
casting aside all ritual and decorum,
to the side of one so hapless, so forlorn,
whose spine bends like a crooked bow,
whose eyes are heavy with fragments,
resting on a crumpled bed,
where the memory of the moment
lingers briefly,
only to vanish again into forgetfulness.

What use is a life like this,
to anyone, for anything?
Rising, piece by piece,
with every ounce of effort,
straightening my spine,
I cross caves, mountains, rivers, and sevenfold realms,
breathless, running through the vast expanse.
In this detached hour,
as I alone know it,
the ultimate outcome of this journey
is painfully clear—
for I am not myself,
not in control of my own being.

Breaking the discipline of all disciplines,
dragged long before birth,
leaping the lines of fate in reckless haste—
why, then, did you arrive here?

Arriving, yet turning midway,
returning home like a weary bird,
its wings trembling in flight,
never once looking back.

Old memories make the heart tremble;
in unknown fear, my whole body shivers.
And all the while,
so much is spoken,
so much discussed
about our fleeting contact.

In the scorching heat of this afternoon,
upon the branches of the Frangipani tree,
I sit alone, my mind heavy with sorrow.
All the branches, the buds, the flowers—
nothing seems visible.

Yet on these branches,
in the cool afternoon breeze,
caught between light and shadow,
a subtle glow persists—
and still, I continue to sit.

Holding onto countless eons,
countless lifetimes,
in some state of restless yearning,

I will sit, watching your path,
watching, waiting, endlessly.

Through countless eons and lifetimes,
as though the event itself is returning home,
I will remain,
yet I will not be there—
I will not be there with you.

In the state of life's nectar,
your body and mind linger near,
like a shade cast,
always present, yet not quite beside me—
as if hovering close,
as my heart feels it to be.

Day by day, through immeasurable pain and toil,
in the sky of fate, like clouds of belief,
my dreams rise and fall, victorious and defeated,
like rippling constellations
in the half-dark of night.

In the invisible, overflowing cosmos,
upon the vast canvas of imagination,
with the brush of some rare master,
moment by moment, life is born anew.

And as I watch, watch,
something forms at the edge of my hand—
some glimmer, some trace,
a presence, a touch,
a fragment of the ineffable.

Across the four directions,
through eighty-four yojanas,
over fourteen worlds,
all is visible in perfect silence.

There is no beginning,
yet no end;
no question arises,
yet no answer comes.

In the gesture of touching the earth,
like a living goddess,
you sit in some luminous circle,
waiting, yet unattached to anyone.

From the fragrance of the lotus at your feet,
rising from the soil to the heavens,
filling the cosmic expanse,
moment by moment,
the universe is saturated with your presence.
Someday, somehow, somewhere,
in an inevitable, extraordinary moment,
I will meet you.

In the honeyed rain of clouds,
in the languid evening,
where night keeps its moist, dark kohl,
across all directions,
in myriad forms and colors,
in touch, in fragrance, in the savor of life itself,
we will meet along this path—
one day, certain and fated.

And that day will come,
and surely it will pass.
Our secret signatures,
the always-open pages of our diary,
will lie exposed before all,
as though the world itself witnesses us.

How timid, how fragile, how helpless we both are,
between birth and death,
like lone, wandering stars.

Within our own bodies, our own weakness,
day after day, month after month,
we endure endless days and nights,
restless, sleepless,
chasing meaningless dreams
only to dream yet again.

(2)
A barren truce—like a fist of ash upon the tongue,
it lies heavy, mute, unmoving.
The doors click shut in this walled-in house,
where each soul drifts, busy with its little errands,
wandering in and out by their own design.

No gaze turns here, no ear bends low—
who has a moment for this forsaken breath?
Yet the lila unfolds, relentless, sly,
its cunning current carrying all things on.

Through this futile span of searching and sleepless hours,
whatever I had earned—armfuls gathered over time—
I gave it all away, poured into your palms.

Tell me, what else remains with me,
what fragment have I hidden, ungiven, from your gaze?

From this twilight-hued, tender flesh
I cut the moon itself, gifting it in selfless love.
I wrung the bones until they yielded
the marrow of blood, the stream of tears,
the nectar of affection, the weight of motherly care—
all that dwelt within my grasp.

And when the last offering was made,
I stood stripped of plenty,
a pauper of the heart,
begging only in the silence of surrender.

In this maze of yearning and fleeting embrace,
the days destined for tomorrow
have already dissolved.
Now the mind stumbles on a single thought—
how shall the last stretch of time be borne?

Even trust in my own self falters,
like a dim flame shivering in its glass,
while the hours drift onward,
unmoored, uncertain, yet unstoppable.

At times, without reason, your words return—
and in your absence they flood me,

a sudden ache that breaks into tears,
blinding every path before me.

So I gather clay in my trembling hands,
raising a fragile temple of earth,
where Radha and Krishna breathe in forms I shape.
And with each fleeting moment of molding,
each curve pressed into soft, yielding soil,
I dwell wholly in you—
living only through the pulse of your memory.

(3)

It's but a tender imagining—
Were you here, draped in Nilambari silk,
your drape brushing like twilight across my brow,
you would softly wipe my face, my restless thoughts.

Wearing blue gems at your throat,
you would draw me close,
binding me in the gentle thread of imagined love.

Half-truth, half-dream,
you would hum a lullaby,
and in its quiet, my heart would tremble,
enchanted by the echo of what would be.

In the realm of presence and absence,
the heart bows not to truth alone,
but to the playful heaps of whispered lies—
like a naughty child, born blind,
feeling the world as a sightless king would.

With every fleeting moment,
the beloved's tender rhythm
beats again and again,
weaving through the soul's quiet chambers,
pulling, teasing,
a soft, relentless enchantment.

More than life, more than breath itself,
the dream-palace of my beloved
sits quietly in the secret heart.

Suddenly it breaks open,
the hidden chest of mysteries flung wide,
and like sudden torrents from a storm-dark sky,
heavy droplets of shadow fall again and again
through long, relentless days—
as if rain, desperate and unyielding,
pours over the clay-floor of a humble hut,
spreading in precise, measured squares.

The news of your coming reached me—
swift as a sudden gust of wind.
What could I do?
No sense, no thought, no presence at all,
like a moment touched by the spirit of ancestors.

Caught in the middle of the road,
I writhed as if struck by an accident of fate.
The word of your arrival
was whispered by some unseen benevolent hand,
slipping softly into my ear,
vanishing as quickly as it came.

After learning when you would arrive,
my eyes, tightly shut, seemed chained in secret.
I strained, every fiber of me, to see your face once,
yet no matter how I tried,
they refused to open.

Tossed in the blaze of longing and ache,
like water slipping through trembling hands,
I broke apart—
a quiet ruin of desire,
scattered in the silent storm of my own yearning.

(4)
Sometimes, before the sun even rises,
on an October morning, drenched in twinkling dewdrops,
I would wander through our courtyard,
plucking flowers of every hue,
without thinking of you.

I don't know why, after so many years,
your absence still floods my memory,
and recalling every word of yours
brings tears, unbidden and relentless—
like a stubborn child crying again and again.

Seeing my face wet with sorrow,
what would the neighbors think?
They would turn a molehill into a mountain.
No matter how I try, I cannot cry freely;

and this inability to weep
leaves me restless and undone.

I hide the tears in the corners of my eyes,
and return home, carrying my grief silently,
a storm of longing contained behind clenched lids.

Sometimes, a strange, stubborn part of my heart
burns and writhes in the scorching afternoon,
trembling without reason,
haunted by your unforgettable, ineffable dusk-like form.

In the distant horizon,
your presence flashes like lightning
through the folds of a georgette sari,
nestled in the embrace of dark, drifting clouds,
under the rumble of thunder and the storm's low chant.

In the shivering creation of a cold breeze,
as clouds scatter above the churn of the sky,
whether you are near me or far,
it feels as if you cling to my body and soul—
again and again.

In the lonely hush of a storm-dark night,
when the mind sits heavy and still,
your presence floods memory,
and through your long absence,
I am haunted by the weight of your words,
aching in the quiet of my solitude.

Are you the cursed, confined script of my life,
a futile chronicle of misfortune?
Are you the silent echo of my every breath,
a proud yet hollow presence in the world,
spinning endlessly in the meaningless cycle of my days,
my golden signature turning in circles,
forever unclaimed, forever alone?

In the sculpted gesture of surrender,
in pure, untamed emotion,
you sit, holding fast through time.
Again and again,
you resonate through the flow of earth and sky,
through the unparalleled rhythms of rivers and mountains,
echoing a spellbound, astonished wonder.

You are the delicate, unmatched sweetness of a raga,
a shimmering, boundless melody,
an eternal, radiant music

I am summoning you—
every day, every hour, every fleeting moment.
Through months of relentless rains,
above the altar of fierce anguish,
in the posture of offering,
amid the sacred logs and all the rites of the fire.

When you arrive, I shall be
half-burning, half-smoldering,
a fragrant incense
in the sacrificial fire of life itself.

In slow, deliberate rhythm,
like a silent, naked dance,
I lie in stillness, my beloved.
O eternal dearest,
I shall honor you from head to toe,
in manifold forms,
painted anew in hue and shape.

With worshipful devotion,
I shall give you life—
woven into the threads of tomorrow,
bound in a garland of stories,
like a goddess enshrined in her image.

As long as you live,
you shall dwell in the cord of my love,
ever entwined, ever cherished.

(5)
Come to me—
first, I will bathe you in scented waters,
infused with aguru and sandal,
letting the fragrance rise like whispered devotion.

Then, from treasures of vibrant hues,
I will adorn you, each piece kissed by light,
every limb shimmering like a diamond,
radiant with the quiet fire of our love.

Come to me—
I will drape your deep-blue, cloud-soft robe
with countless jasmine blooms,
and around your neck,
I will place a pearl garland of trust and devotion,
woven with faith and gentle care.

I will steep you in the color of desire,
tracing your form with kohl-dark longing.
Your two unforgettable, innocent blue eyes—
a canvas of endless wonder.

I will crown your nose with a jewel,
your arms with diamond-studded bangles,
ears aglow with rubies and glittering earrings,
your forehead bathed in the crimson light of sunset.

On your red-tinged feet,
I will weave sixty-four intricate designs,
each stroke deep, each hue alive,
as if painted by a master's loving hand,
an ode to your radiant, eternal beauty.

On your soft, almond-hued lips,
tinged with honeyed blooms,
I will place a kiss.
In the sweetness of our longing,
in the jasmine-scented dusk,
our final union shall unfold,
fearless and complete.

We will walk, unbound,
under the open sky of autumn,
where every step is touched by the season's golden glow,
and every moment hums with the song of us.

In every drop of sweat and tear,
I will paint the image of Radha and Krishna
upon your glittering chest.

Shy and drenched in the moment,
you will watch as I trace each curve—
the perfect, tender swell of your bosom,
hair rising like whispers along your skin,
again and again,
in the sacred rhythm of devotion and desire.

Tonight marks the uncertain union
of our cursed tomorrow—
this night, this very night, and no other.
Tomorrow brings only frayed anguish,
inauspicious omens, fearful shadows.

When our night touches the small earth,
an entire age will have passed in stillness.
After that long, silent age,
what fate awaits this wretched one?
Whether fortune will smile or not—
who can ever know?

(6)
I keep whispering, "Tomorrow night will pass,"
not knowing when it truly will.

Once this night fades away,
tomorrow holds no words to speak.

Your secret, held in silent solitude,
I long to utter, again and again—
yet each day it lingers,
unvoiced,
a soft ache humming in the stillness of my heart.

You hover around me like storm-dark clouds,
heavy with sorrow, playful in their shrouds.
Silent you come, silent you go,
slipping through corners I'll never know.

Even as I stretch my hand to the sky,
across the vast, unfeeling high,
I cannot touch you, cannot hold—
you remain just beyond my grasp,
a distant flame in my longing soul.

Whether I touch your dusky grace or not,
in anxious longing the night slips by unseen.
Each passing hour dissolves into torment,
every moment shredding my life thread by thread.

Your body—so flawless, your face—
a goddess-image beyond all words.
Yet at times, like ghost or devil in your whim,
you make me dance, day and night,
in a ceaseless, smokeless fire.
Adorned in all finery and ornament,
wherever you may be,

do not delay—come swiftly.
And in the deep sweetness of longing,
press one last kiss upon my parched lips.

Gazing upon this unadorned, bare face,
you may whisper,
"See how faded, how pale it looks."
Yet know that once, this face, this mouth,
was yours alone—
more precious than life or death,
tender and irresistible.

Like a life bound within the petals of a flower,
my being is laid bare for you,
and I wait—blind, like a patient creator,
again and again,
restless, desperate,
trembling with the ache of longing.

(7)
Tonight is the endless night of a million imaginings,
the final union of our boundless longing.
This night is all that is—tomorrow shall not be.
When the cursed night of tomorrow
arrives upon our world,
how many ages, how many lifetimes
will have slipped by in its passing?

This merciless, unbridled time waits for no one,
racing like a swift, untamed steed along its path.
In the colorful festival of love and compassion,
like a goddess,

you will appear, distant yet vividly present.
We will have already consumed that vision,
and only the memory of its ecstasy will remain,
until the final meeting of life and tomorrow comes.

And yet, in the quiet between,
I wonder—
will you be able to leave from here,
before the final embrace,
before the ultimate union that time itself delays?

When, at last, you arrive unexpectedly,
shall we sit awake through the night for each other?
All these years, it has lain open, unclaimed,
and when the hour comes to gather and depart,
we will follow our separate paths.

Time slips through our hands,
Taking all we wish to hold.
Amid the crowd, your fair face may vanish from my sight.
Before dawn, each ornament will be laid out,
from crown to toes, waiting for you.
One by one, you will adorn yourself,
watching your chest, lips, and face,
and in that quiet, unfamiliar wonder,
I will tremble, helpless, in awe.

Until the festival ends, age upon age may pass,
yet here I will remain, head bowed,
savoring the tender ache,
immersed in the slow, sacred rhythm of longing,

where every pause, every glance,
is a gentle song to the heart.

As time quietly slips away,
so too your body and soul shiver again and again,
like soft leaves trembling in the breeze.

In this state, you will hold me tight—
around the waist, along the back—
while one streak of me remains,
like an old, worn cloth, lying bare and still.

In the shadowed corners of this house,
our future will flutter endlessly,
like pages of an old calendar,
mouths agape, turning year after year.

In this twinkling, restless home,
days and nights pass in silent turmoil,
where the paths of our coming and going
seem to mirror one another,
folded into the quiet rhythm of longing.

What is day, what is night—
as though seven thousand dawns and dusks
have pressed their weight upon the hours.

In the crush of the crowd,
yesterday flickers and fades,
and all things come to an end—

like a train pausing at a nameless halt,
in a village barren and still,
where silence grows like dust.

(8)
I know—your being or not being
was never a possibility in destiny.

Whatever was meant to happen
was fulfilled ages ago,
one by one,
like chapters closed in silence.

Everywhere the world stands still—
miles and miles of unmoving quiet.

Like drops trembling
on a lotus leaf,
you—
and I, stubborn in my own path,
break apart
like deep green waves
in unspoken agony.

Then the mind sways—
a little steady, a little restless,
like a fool, impoverished,
fallen in a scattered house.

The seer of the future
offers small consolations,

yet the script of birth—
its karmic burden—
must be lived.

All this was inscribed
long ago,
in an unfathomable time.

This voiceless fool—
tasting the essence of secrets,
as if understanding, yet never understanding.

At times mute, at times deaf,
then drifting,
like a torn boat floating
in water still, then suddenly restless.

And yet, for ages unveiled,
a frail body of only seventy hands' span,
soft, ungraspable—
like weeds:
sometimes fresh,
sometimes withered,
yet always rooted, unmoving,
unyielding.

If it is to be the last time,
then come once—
look once more
at what was once so dear to you,
so much your own.

What was this body—
and what has it become in a few short days?

Like an ancient document,
half seen, half erased,
bearing the faded mark
of a broken signature.

At times I writhe in longing,
so weary, so unsettled—
on a heated afternoon,
or when, in late August,
a chain of dark clouds
breaks into rain across the courtyard,
your memory strikes me,
wild and unbearable.

What am I,
with this strange destiny of mine—
ever in my own control?

In the August rains,
in the breath that halts,
staggering, as the wind passes through,
I watch the crystal walls
of my self-belief shatter before my eyes.

The river of dreams leaps across its banks,
flowing in dazzling, thundering dance.
And I—like a leaf adrift,
floating in floodwaters,
belong neither here
nor there.

(9)

Night upon night, etched with stars and planets—
a silent, sapphire night,
not a festival of delight,
but a night of grief,
a night of Mahakal.

Beneath the shimmering canopy
of an unfathomed sky,
your radiant face appears—
so pale, so sorrowful,
half in shadow,
half lit by the fragile glow of the moon.

Like a kasatandi flower,
your whitened visage gleams—
is it truly yours,
or someone else's?
Even to recognize it feels uncanny.

After decades have slipped away,
in the age beyond forty,
you appear like clouds adrift—
sometimes broken, fragmented,
ashen and worn;
sometimes drenched,
kohl-dark, luminous, pure,
against the deep of night.

And in the solitary hours,
in the voiceless rooms,
I can neither live without you
nor die in your absence.

Like one undone,
trapped in decay,
I wander the strange road
between memory and forgetting.

The unforgotten memory
of a sorrowful past
burns through every moment—
like a sharp, polished blade
piercing flesh and soul.

A slender body,
a little dusky, fragile,
turns to ashes in the fire of longing,
before my very eyes.

Yet from the sacrificial fire of faith
I rise again,
searching and searching
for my place,
my ground,
and with each step of renewal
I declare my being anew.

We two—
not in words, not in idle talk—
misunderstanding each other,

walk astray upon some unreachable path,
drifting back and forth, barren and weary.

You and I—
like wanderers upon an unknown, strange road,
roaming here and there, beggars of the day,
from dawn till dusk.

Deliberately,
we let whole wasted years slip away,
lost, forgotten.

Wherever I turn,
your shadowed memories bind me
into a depth of emotion—
like blue Aparajita blossoms,
layer upon layer of petals,
a sea of indigo.

Sometimes, like a torn kite,
I waver—
rising, falling beneath the endless sky,
while a gentle Gandharva raga drifts,
soft, sweet,
lingering somewhere,
flowing through days and nights unceasingly
without our knowing.

Countless births,
countless deaths—
in earlier lives, I have borne
my own fate,

my own karmic fruits,
in astonishment, in sorrowful wonder.

Now, the thin wick of this lamp of life,
unlit, begins to fade—
along the alleys of dawn,
beside the river's edge.

In the desolate graveyard,
as your garments, one by one,
cling to dust and soil,
some bewildered, ruined ascetic—
a shattered kapalik—
must have sat in restless wonder,
gazing at your half-worn, half-fallen robe,
beneath the startled moonlight
of the last autumn night.

(10)

The season of renunciation—
autumn.

The season of detached unions—
autumn.
The season where desire blooms,
fragile as flowers—
autumn.
The season of the languid maiden,
innocent yet unyielding—
autumn.
The merciless season—
autumn.

On autumn's scentless, wandering night,
I shall wither—
like the Brahmakamal,
folding back into silence.

But you, beloved,
must go—
go where the path calls you,
back to the realm
from which you once arrived.

All the sins and virtues you gathered—
bind them now,
wrap them within the folds
of your own night-worn veil,
and take them with you.

Go.
Go, leaving behind
the crippled old master,
the helpless son and daughter-in-law,
the breath of the village,
and the unlettered sister-in-law
to whom you told so many lies.

Go swiftly,
and let the remaining days
be lived in laughter and ease.

Go—
go without fear,
go into freedom.

In the deep, dark hours of night,
you arrive here—
then, at the crossroads, lose your way,
wandering into shadow.

All that has happened
in the paths of coming and going—
let it not break you.
Forget pride, forget resentment;
press forward, onward—
your fate, your destiny,
like a speeding train,
leaping from station to station.

Hurry, for this is
the ruthless politics of time.

After you left,
some painter,
with stale, crushed liquids,
drew your tiny Laxmi-prints
all over the house.

Outside,
he adorned the space
with Madhumalti blossoms,
a Kelikunj,
a mansion of imagination,
in the silent realms of Alkapuri.

Countless forgotten, famous,
and nameless faces,

piled in deep-blue waves of hair,
in the hues of night,
thick, spiraling, crimson,
touched your luscious lips.

The Time of Departure

When the hour of departure comes,
who can ever hold it back?

What must occur
will unfold, even in delay.
What is destined to break
will fracture—by carelessness,
by the silent hand of fate.

Like crystal shards
in a frozen winter night,
each nerve, each goosebump
becomes a sharp, burning point.

The body, crimson and bruised,
blood flowing like molten rivers,
breath surging upward, fierce and wild,
the throat parched, clinging,
as pain threads through every vein,
an unstoppable, vivid ache
etched in the marrow of night.

When the hour of departure comes,
a soul mounts an elephant,
a horse, a motor scooter,

or rides a train into the distance—
bearing sorrow,
folded quietly into the folds of their clothing,
carrying grief as a silent companion.

Brothers, friends, companions,
those familiar, those barely known,
will weep a little,
watch them fade along the path,
then, absorbed in the rhythm of their own lives,
forget—
as the world moves on,
leaving only the whisper of absence behind.

Ah! That poor soul, departing—
riding a motorbike,
passing lines of trees, poles,
catching glimpses of familiar faces—
suddenly struck by wonder.

Hands pressed to the forehead,
he silently curses his own fate,
muttering in his mind,
as the world drifts past,
and he rides on alone.

While departing, I saw her face—
how it had fallen,
her small, dark eyes
wilted beneath the weight of silent anguish.

From her lips,

all laughter seemed to have been stolen,
and her fair skin
was drained and dry
under the relentless burn of sorrow.

She wished to speak,
to utter a thousand words,
yet nothing came —
only silence remained.

I left her there, alone,
and rode away on my broken motorbike.

Neighbours linger,
sharing in my sorrow.
On the courtyard floor,
a blue shadow spreads across my body,
and blood flows,
gently collected
into a shattered bottle.

What is the hurry?
What gain comes
from remembering
the hiding place of a restless soul?

What gain comes
from mounting a doubtful wooden horse,
and wandering the city streets
in endless circles?
All lies, all falsehoods —
what is wrong becomes right.

What is brought,
is brought from the same place
from which it came.

Birth and death—
they are not separate.
Truth is eternal.

Rubi, dear!
This is our final mark,
the seal of life and death,
our true identity.

What Feelings Stir

In the quiet delay of receiving Rubi's letter,
as the postman's hour slips by,
and the temple bell tolls,
in the corners of the courtyard,
a figure appears—
his eyes heavy with sadness,
his face dried and weary,
bearing the weight of longing.

Nothing in words can hold the mind today.
Arranging the drawing room,
applying cold cream,
gazing at one's own face in the mirror—
all seems hollow.

Light an incense stick,
kneel down,
and offer a silent prayer to God,
seeking solace beyond the restless heart.

It feels strange,
not hearing from her,
the delay in meeting.

The mind stirs, tempted—
a wooden doll,
held only in this fragile trust,
perhaps, somehow,
will melt
into my palm.

Who Will Mend The Heart

Who will love me tenderly,
caress my hair,
press their lips to mine,
and stay awake through endless nights,
telling tales of kings,
softly easing my restless heart?

Who is here for me,
to weep in my sorrow,
to melt into laughter and joy,
becoming one with me?

Around me, darkness spreads,
thick and unbroken,
while the vigilant hands of time
strike out their endless, varied chords.

Am I but a corpse?
Through countless nights, I have become
a living corpse,
my body surrounded
by mountains and valleys,
resonating with the sacred sounds of Ram's name.

I have cut all bonds and slept,
like Kumbhkarna, upon a jeweled bed.
Who is here, truly mine,
to let this river of blood flow?

Alone,
like meaningless letters echoing
through the void,
I count,
watching the silence unfold.

This luminous land—
one kingdom, one king,
one sound, no other.
All words stripped of meaning,
all language a hollow riddle.

If today my Rubi were seated beside me,
held gently in the palms of my hands,
her small, laughing mouth
singing like a little parrot
a clear, sweet song of devotion—

I would lift her onto my head, O Lord,
blessing her again and again,
hanging the garlands of her virtues around her neck,
and every morning and evening
we would rise with hymns and music,
singing praises in joyous devotion.

I do not seek rebirth,
nor the throne of heaven,
nor a seat of diamonds, pearls, and sapphires.

All I ask of You, O Lord,
is that my Rubi may live long.
Let the vast, dark dominion
stay far from the sky of her mind,
shielding her from shadow and sorrow.

Since you left

After you left, all became desolate.
The air smells of gunpowder from distant planes,
everything blurred—inside the house, outside.

No crowd stirs within the walls,
no tinkling of cups to break the silence.
The night stretches endlessly,
and I swing in the cradle of emptiness,
awake through countless hours,
counting the stars in the sky.

Like a greedy merchant,
a faint longing stirs within me,
quiet, restless, hungry.

After you departed, all became unsettled—
books and clothes scattered in every direction,
life itself split in two,
as sharp as a knife's edge.

The dim city hums with silent torment,
telephone wires tremble like restless wings,
and memories soar,
an eagle riding the currents of my mind.

After you left, merciless time arrived —
terrible unease,
a hidden fire of invisible pain
burning in the blood of restless thought.

Secret forces, subtle agents of torment,
weaving skillful threads of sorrow,
fill this life to the brim
with grief, remorse, and lament.

All around, only fatigue and defeat
stretch across the world.

After you left,
this house remained unchanged —
a silent festival of bodiless souls,
wandering through day and night.

Curtains flutter in the restless wind,
and under unseen, potent forces,
the house has become
a crematorium in my eyelids,
where unbroken emptiness
reigns supreme.

Not like before —
6 a.m. tea,
now eludes me.

Under the bed lamp,
entwined in the mosquito net,

sleep will not come,
restless and tight.

As I leave for meetings, committees,
no one stirs with the same intensity as you.
And watching the path you will return by,
I neither rage nor persist—
the stubborn fire of desire quiets itself.

After you left,
I am no longer as I was—
the mischief has faded.
I no longer break cups,
nor scold the servants.

At the front door,
I do not knock, calling for you.
I no longer watch the clock,
returning home at the perfect hour.

After you left,
everything fell apart.
The house fills with spiderwebs and soot,
books scattered across the floor,
clothes, notes, half-used cosmetics—
all in disarray.

In the mirror,
sometimes your face flashes,
sudden and vivid,
like a goddess appearing.
As if you are here—

yet you are not.
Bound within the tight confines of time.

Why, in this causeless emptiness,
does a human burn so fiercely,
consumed by the disappearance
of their own beloved presence?

Clutching handfuls of sorrow,
they scatter themselves
into the winds,
tugging at the garden of flowers,
striking the trees with violent force,
as blossoms and fruit fall
and branches break.

Why does such utter loneliness spread,
like shadows threading through blood and sinew,
when one stares death in the face?

And death, silent and patient,
completes its work without a word,
leaving only
the vast, unbroken void
to cradle what once was.

Jealousy

In her hands, the glittering red bangles
Steal away my senses—
I cannot fathom how,
But with the arrival of the moonlit night,
Every drop of my blood
Begins to wander restlessly.

At the curve of her dusky lips,
A flicker of laughter glimmers—
And like Bijigupta, desire surges in me,
Until I dissolve into air.

The strangest wonder remains:
I am Ruby's first and final lover,
Spending nights with torches lit within my bones.
Each day, like a sorrow-drunken Madhav,
I wait in the depths of her entwining vines.

Vision within Vision

A decade gone—
since I left Rubi's city,
its lanes—familiar, unfamiliar—
still breathe in me.

In drains and broken corners
envy collects,
hatred drips,
longing waits,
desire gleams in market stalls.

And in the water,
a bitter line remains—
like an arrow, sharp,
etched deep,
unwilling to fade.

The distance is not so great,
yet I, like a sleepless wanderer,
keep losing count.

Time stretches in the forest
like a python winding through trees.

And in the night,
close to my ear,
I hear—
his breath,
loud, insistent—
presence turned absence,
nearness made far.

Ten years have passed—
yet Rubi's city clings to me
like an unhealed scar.

Its alleys rise in memory,
bus stands breathing with crowds,
walls once plastered with red and blue notices—
perhaps by now torn away,
lifted into the sky as kites
by restless boys.

I imagine the city still trembling,
restless with secrets
only the night can keep.

In the final hours before dawn
your silence comes,
piercing deeper than words—
a venom threading through my veins,
leaving me helpless,
like a child
crying into emptiness.

And then—
a fistful of nothingness,
a gust of bitter air,
a loneliness without end
fills my blood.

You strip me hollow,
turn me into a heretic
before my own faith.
The idols are stolen
again and again from the temple.

And far away,
on Dadhinauti peak,
the eagle beats its wings—
a sound like thunder—
echoing across a land
drowned in desolation.

Silence will wave its hand again and again,
its charm wilting, slackening.

Eyes will turn bloodless,
like frost over a frozen pane,
while handfuls of emptiness
shower down—
petals of jasmine,
your body, your breath,
rising and falling
like incense on smoldering sandalwood,
untamed, fragrant, untamed as ever.

I stand like a detached ascetic,
gazing at your face
as a devotee might,
with tear-filled eyes.

Two deep, dark orbs—
like twin pillars of dawn,
anchored to the Arun Stambh,
holy, unyielding,
holding me in silent reverence,
while the world drifts away.

Close Enough to Feel

How close we are,
How far apart too,
How much distance lies within our souls.
From earth to sky, and sky to earth again,
Everywhere — only gloom and darkness,
A blue tapestry woven with pain.

You — the Woman, I — the Seer.
I dwell in your imagined divinity;
our love, our remembrance, our promise —
a rare echo of a vanished century.

You build walls around me,
raising embankments of contact,
while I create you anew,
swimming through the river of faith.
Who knows where either of us belong?
In dreams within dreams,
our world is born —
out of a beautiful misunderstanding.
We two lose ourselves —
as if we must be lost in each other.
All sorrow will dissolve;
we shall no longer remain upon this earth,
no trace, no hue of our existence.

In the faded, foggy forest —
lie the helpless remains
of a dead poet from a dead century.

Riverbank

One day I wandered, hurried,
to a silent, untimely shore —
not a riverbank, but a misplaced destiny.
The one I first beheld there,
I had seen ages ago,
countless times upon some unseen road,
in that delicate instant
before a dream shatters.

Who did I meet in that abandoned house of echoes?
A stubborn, beloved companion?
Or my first and final love,
or a vision born from some crystal city of imagination?
Let them be who they may,
yet why do they come here,
to this silent, deserted shore?

They arrived quietly,
like a goddess at the sacred hour of ritual ablution,
glimmering with inner light.
Their presence burned like a procession of flames,
eyes like hidden forests reflecting untold depths,
skin soft as moonlit petals,
trembling like banyan leaves in the wind,
a form that spoke of delicate beauty,

a vision at once tangible and ethereal.
Who, but a goddess, could appear thus,
and who else could one behold in such radiant grace?

One day, at the silent riverbank, we met —
fate's quiet decree beneath the misted dawn.
But our meeting stirred the village air,
whispers weaving through streets and courtyards,
colored murmurs dancing in the throng.
Small traders glimpsed sparks of our secret,
and in the tide of chatter, our bond
bloomed into scandal, yet the river alone
kept the truth shimmering beneath its silver skin.

And seeing her, what is she to me?
Without her, how many days stretch between us,
how many months, how many years?
Or is she a companion across lifetimes,
and, in the quiet intimacy of souls,
my closest sister of the heart?

Perhaps, in some past life,
by the merit of good deeds,
I became bound to her love,
like a shadow following light.
Yet, have I ever truly met her in a dream?

If it was my fate to endure so much sorrow,
without fault of my own,
if all of life and death were to pass
like a play upon the cosmic stage,
and there was no other way —

would someone not whisper to me,
"Enough, dear one, be ready to go"?

All my life I gave in vain,
performing acts of charity and duty,
yet what remains to offer her now?
I have sat, waiting, ready all this while,
and still, the question lingers: am I ready?"
At the turning of the world's alleys —
a night struck down —
my hand crushed as I fell; was she ever truly near?
That champak-barani charuhasini —
did she ever stand by me?
And yet she came to the silent riverbank each instant,
never clasping my palm, but raking me with her talons.

Along invisible lanes where lightning weeps, she walked —
why such hardship to arrive at my shadowed shore ?

O sarbomanoharini, labanyabarnini, mrugakhi tribalasobhini,
niloptala padmamukhi, padmanayani!
If by tantra and black mantra they conjured this nocturne of breath,
if in some hidden shrine she worshipped to make me forget,
she came at the very hour I was to depart.

But why this untimely coming — an old devil's step —
to the lonely riverbank, as if to sip the last red of my blood?

Hermitage

Hesitant at first — to go, or yet remain —
then I slipped from the house,
stepping straight into the path.

Day by day, night by night, I had woven
gardens of bloom and fruit,
sweet labyrinths of my own making —
all forgotten in a single heartbeat.

The pension book, the bank passbook,
my mother's black-and-white face, tilak-marked,
my ailing wife's prescriptions since birth,
her hands holding mine with gentle love,
Odisha Sahitya Akademi's plaque,
all the sealed deeds of paternal inheritance —
left behind, like whispers in the wind.

Like a wandering butterfly a lone butterfly,
I floated from the house,
leaving all anchors, all proofs, all care,
carrying only the pulse of the heart,
drifting into the unknown,
into the silent, endless air.

Along the paths of coming and going,
through every turn, every rise and fall,
I met countless souls —
yet often I turned my face, unseen, unnoticed,
and walked on.

Where I stumbled, where I was caught —
what thought held me there?
Had I decided, in some quiet corner of the heart,
that I was meant to remain?
Had I willed it, I would not have stalled on the road;
I would have pressed onward- anger my only compass-
to find your house and leave it burning in my wake.

Your house is sunk in some strange metal,
an alloy forged to hide and hold —
no matter how I seek that city, your house
will not yield itself to my finding.

How then shall I learn the full address of your home?
The very house whose place I once forgot on purpose-
can that hidden place be found so easily now?
Is a forgetting I planted myself so simple to undo?

Each time I sent a letter to the wrong address,
it returned to me,
marked absent,
as if the world itself conspired
to keep my words from reaching you.

Had your address been etched in my memory,
I would not have lingered at the square before the square,

nor paused beside that two-storied house.
I would have summoned the
neighbours like secret-keepers,
drawn the path from their lips like whispered maps,
then crossed the threshold of your courtyard,
pushed open the gate,
and met you first —
before the world could speak your name.

Before I could meet you,
I encountered the one who knew you best — your closest friend.
With gentle urgency, she whispered,
"Go, go to the one you seek so madly;
her house stands just across from mine."

I followed her words like a secret map,
and arrived at your home —
the house of unspoken echoes,
where time itself seemed to hold its breath.

There you lay,
left hand tucked beneath your head,
face turned southward,
crumpled in the quiet rapture of sleep.
You dreamed in a world of your own,
silent, withdrawn,
and I, standing after so many days,
felt the weight of centuries in your glance.

Yet when you saw me,
it was as if I were nothing —

a shadow on the threshold of your life,
and you turned your face away,
guarding your solitude,
as though our long ache had been
no more than a fleeting dream.

In dreams, sometimes she laughed,
sometimes she wept, speaking softly to someone unseen.
I did not call her by name,
nor revealed the hiding place of my own heart.

I sat quietly by her side,
as her white hair lifted gently in the air,
stirred by some tender, invisible wind.
I dared not touch,
yet watched as she moved slowly,
breathing in rhythms I could only fear to name.

Her inhale, her exhale,
each rise and fall of her chest —
I trembled at the sheer intimacy of it,
lost in the silent, sacred terror of witnessing her soul.

Hands unmoving,
they lay there — like a living corpse,
or like one transported on some strange, light-
ning-etched ornamental chariot
from an unknown planet.

In gestures, in glances with a dark, ugly Brahman,
how much was being said?
Or like eagles circling a fallen body,

they sat among relatives,
listening to tales of devils beneath the ocean's waters.

Or perhaps, along the path between worlds,
they themselves became
the miracle of new consciousness,
a story born of their own being,
alive with its own luminous, strange wonder.

Will You Go Once?

When he left the village,
how old could that boy have been?
Eleven—perhaps twelve at most.
A face too young for a beard,
too innocent for deceit,
too untouched to know
what love or attachment truly mean.

In those tender years,
he never imagined
he would one day leave behind
the Dalamakudi games by the forest's edge,
the canal that kissed his father's fertile fields,
the morning khichdi bhog of Kartik,
the fading walls of the temple of Sri Radhakrishna,
adorned once with mango-flower garlands,
and the drifting songs of wind
that wandered through his quiet village.

He could not have known
that someday,
he would have to leave it all behind.

When he left,
the rarest treasures stayed behind —

those small, irreplaceable things
that time cannot recreate.

The black-and-white photograph
where his parents smiled together,
a few worn books whispering his name,
his grandmother's clay piggy bank
still echoing with saved dreams,
and Jhunu Didi's sky-coloured sweater,
woven with warmth,
threaded with love.

None of it he carried.
He came away empty-handed —
as though memory itself
had become too fragile to hold.

All the days he lived here,
a fatherless child
in a narrow, rented room of this street,
he kept remembering—
day and night—
the faces of his childhood friends:
Kirtika, Jubula, Bishnu, Basanti,
and dear Jhunu Didi.

Their laughter wandered through his dreams,
their voices echoed
in the still corners of his solitude.

Kirtika —
twice fallen in the fifth,

left his lessons mid-way,
like an unfinished song.
One bright March day,
the priest read the stars —
a good moment, he said —
and they tied him to another fate.
Soon he was a father,
his laughter folded
into the hum of days.

Bishnu, Jubula —
gone from the schoolyard,
gone from the dust and the mango shade.
One dissolved into distance,
one into silence —
no letter,
no echo,
no trace of return.

Better not to speak
of the girl next door —
the one with the proud eyes
and moonlit airs.

They say she fell in love
with Prafulla Bhanja,
the contractor from Barijanga —
too soon, too young.
One night,
beneath the hospital's white silence,
her story ended before it began.

By dawn,
Basanti was gone —
vanished with a distant relative,
Suryabandhu Bhai,
to faraway Rourkela —
leaving behind
only whispers,
and the faint scent
of rain on her window.

And Jhunu Didi?
She was six, perhaps seven years older —
yet to me,
no one in the whole wide world
was as beautiful as she.
Grace in her body,
light in her hands,
a nose sharp as a parrot's beak,
eyes that spoke more than words could dare.
Her hair — dark as storm clouds,
her face — bright as a goddess's dawn.

Anyone who saw her
paused for a breath,
lost between awe and silence.
How strange —
that she, of all the world,
should pour such affection
into a fatherless child like me.

Clad in a white sari,
the colour of moonlight,

Jhunu Didi came —
in the blazing June noon,
to the house where the child lay asleep.

Her cheeks flushed like a red hibiscus,
her lips soft and gleaming like butter,
her forehead trembling
with an unknown fear.

She held him close to her chest —
and wept, silently,
as if her heart were unravelling
in the heat and light.

When he stirred,
wondering what had happened,
she was gone —
gone like a storm,
as swiftly as she came,
leaving behind
the scent of hibiscus
and an emptiness that never spoke again.

From that day,
whispers began to stir —
soft at first,
then swirling, spreading —
from one lip to another,
from one courtyard to the next,
until the whole village
hummed with rumour.

In the meeting hall,
voices rose like dust in summer wind.
Without proof,
without witness,
they cast all blame
upon the boy —
and upon his widowed mother.

Tears fell like offerings of defeat
as they were told to leave.
And so, weeping,
they walked away from the village —
two shadows
crossing the border of belonging.

It feels as if it were only yesterday,
yet fifty years have passed
within the blink of this long silence.

The village —
once drawn clear in memory's map —
must have changed by now,
its lanes grown wild with time.

But the scar of that old sorrow
still burns upon the man's body,
as if carved by fate itself.
Even after half a century,
the boy within him
cannot forget his village —
nor the whispers
that chased him from its heart.

Why would he go now,
after all these years?
What remains in that far-off village—
Kirtika, Jubula, Bishnu, Basanti…
and Jhunu Didi—
where are they now?

Who waits there for him,
to hear his untold truth,
to see his innocence
that no one cared to see then?

Why would he walk those lanes again,
where even the dust remembers his tears?
Why return so late,
to a place that forgot
yet still lives within him?

Enchantress

Why have you come,
so late in the season—
is there still something left unsaid,
something time forgot to erase?

The pages of years have turned to dust,
yet one mark still bleeds unhealed.
Did the wind that stopped
when I left the world,
carry your voice—
or silence it forever?

All my life,
I wandered —
like a beggar without a name,
seeking warmth in the dust of days.

Now, I remain
the same beggar still —
but what I had,
all I ever owned,
I had already given you —
long before desire learned to speak.

From every vein,
I poured out my blood for you —

weighed in silence
the flesh of this dusky body,
and gave that too.

I offered the priceless gifts
of affection, love, and motherly warmth —
gave you my love,
and in the folds of my being,
offered shelter — fearless,
filled with hope and trust.

Having offered all,
the beggar stayed —
empty-handed, yet full of love.

Just now,
He stepped out, ready to leave,
To a place unknown,
Its every corner hidden from me.

Do I know where?
Like a shadow,
I follow him, suffocated, running,
chasing him every step.

Why do you search
for the secret corners of that place,
and depart so fiercely?

Where will you go —
where will he vanish to?

Long before you arrived,
the hour of my leaving
had quietly taken shape.

All the rare treasures of life
were gathered to accompany me:
tilak mingled with camphor and agaru
a whisper of Ganga water,
marigolds glowing like caught sunlight,
a pinch of mahaprasad,
crumbled nirmalya,
sandalwood sticks steeped in scent,
a cloth pale as moonlight,
and a simple stretcher
waiting to bear me away.

Baked in the sun,
like a deity awaiting worship,
why did you come at such a time?

Halfway along the path,
to distract me,
to torment me
in some unseen hell?

All my life,
like repeated offerings to Shree Devi,
my body laid bare,
my being yielded,
and you took everything —
my very essence,
my all.

Were you my foe from lives before,
that you returned —
one final time —
only to torment me again?

You granted me neither peace in life,
nor rest in death;
you stood between my breath and my silence,
my birth and my release.

In A Crowd

In forty long years, not once
Did our paths truly meet —
Not at a festival, not at a feast,
Not even in the silence of farewell rites.

Through these four decades,
We kept walking our separate ways —
For the love we bore was strange,
A tale that ended
Before it ever began…

Like autumn rain —
Damp, wistful, and unfinished —
Falling softly on a memory
That never found its season.

Forty years have slipped by,
As strangers, we have watched time pass.
In this span, countless unseen turns
Have unfolded before our eyes —
Unexpected, unbelievable, yet real.

From school and college days,
So many dear friends have faded away;
That one rival who never liked me,

Those jealous kin who smiled in pretense —
All have taken leave,
Walking their own destined paths.

Through wars, bloodshed, and explosions in vain,
The meaning of life itself
Has quietly transformed —
Changed beyond all recognition,
Like a river that forgot
Where it first began to flow.

In the restless twilight of autumn,
I wandered — like a ghost,
Haunting street after silent street —
From the temple to the Ramakrishna Math,
And sometimes into that forsaken shrine
Where dust sleeps on broken idols.

Like a rootless, dying tree
Before sinking its teeth into the earth,
Did I not sit there — aching, waiting —
Just once more
To see your face,
Radiant with that quiet grace

So much crowd, so much noise —
Yet not a single known face in sight.
The air hums with strangers' voices,
And I stand — an echo, not a name.

That chapter,
Which ended before it began,
Lies sealed in the dust of time.

No dawn awaits its pages now,
No ink shall wake its dreams —
Only silence turns the leaf,
Whispering what might have been.

Why did I come to this place in such bitter time?
The one I sought
Through tear-filled eyes in the crowd —
Where had they gone?

Had they vanished into some shattered orbit,
Or slipped into an ancient ruin,
Or a perilous, forgotten tunnel?
Or perhaps
Perched atop the grey mountain peaks,
Watching silently from afar?

You didn't know, did you?
How long they had been waiting there,
While I wandered, searching
Through the fragments of a lost world.

Who are you searching for here,
In this crowd,
Amid all this laughter and cheer?

The one you seek,
Was it caught once between two lines

Of an unfinished poem,
Stuck in a fleeting disaster of a moment?

You search for them in the throng,
Yet you came here on purpose —
So late,
As if to meet what was already lost.

One Day At Night

One day and night,
After swallowing Alprox,
She turned north and slept,
While I faced south.

But could she truly rest in peace?
Unable to find sleep, she leaned against the wall,
Growing only more desperate.

What happened next — I do not know.
Like a stubborn child, she began to weep,
And in doing so,
Tore apart the fragile sleep I held.

It was her age-old habit,
And she knew my restless temper well.
I watched her tear-streaked face for a while,
Saying nothing,
A slow fire burning inside me,
Like a half-charred log smoldering alone.

Before the night passed,
She left her home —
Wife, son, daughter-in-law, grandchildren — all behind.
Into a dense forest she wandered,

To a graveyard where devils might dwell,
Beneath a banyan tree's thick, whispering leaves,
Like a directionless bird,
Seeking a fleeting rest.

Yet even there, leaving that rare beauty behind,
She could not find peace.
After thirty-three years together,
Under one roof, I never imagined,
That the lady sleeping northward
Could have been both my lover and my wife.

In the abandoned temple,
Like the goddess never worshipped
She would appear each night before me,
Bangles jingling,
A sound that stirred my heart,
And lingered,
Every single night.

Perhaps her days remained,
As a deity's, in some distant realm,
And if it were her destiny to spend them with me,
I would have plunged every time
Into the lake of her crimson lips,
After each sunset.

If the words that flowed from her mouth
Could set the surrounding heavens astir,
If in her tender, motherly touch,
In her sacred presence,
A desolate world could bloom anew —

Then why had she lain so long,
Like a captive spirit,
Half in the shadow of merciless autumn,
Half in the fragile light of dawn?

That night, seeing her in the form of a goddess,
I stood confused, trembling between faith and fear.
Then, gathering strength, burning like fire,
I kept gazing into her two green eyes.

O doe-eyed one, destroyer of illusion, remover of sin!
O Bhadra, savior of worlds, purifier divine!

If in this sorrow and silent grief,
Your every breath was slowing, fading —
If the blend of presence and absence
Had made life itself unbearable —

If my leaving was destined
For your goddess-form to rise,
You could have told me once before…
Then I wouldn't have stayed here —
Ashamed, helpless,
Lying beneath your divine gaze.

Now I look at you,
And I cannot tell —
Are you an angel,
Or a devil cloaked in light?
Only you would know —
Who you truly are.

Today, She Arrives

Tonight is her coming.

She said she would come —
Forgetting all pride, all propriety,
Defying the ancient codes and customs
That bound her kind for ages.

Deceiving husband, mother-in-law,
Sister-in-law, brother-in-law —
She slipped away in silence,
Through the crowded mist of night,

And came, unseen,
Into this dense forest —
Where shadows breathe,
And forbidden dreams take shape.

I have come —
Yet there is no sound of her,
No vision, no sign.

The mingled scent of sandal and moonlight,
Once rising from her skin,
No longer drifts
Through the tangle of vines.

Among fallen leaves,
No anklet rings beneath her steps;
Around me, no sacred circle glows
With her presence or her absence.

From the grove,
No love-lorn flute sighs its melody,
And the banks of dark-blue Yamuna
Lie undecorated — no festival of immersion tonight.

In this lifeless, bloodless body,
I cannot tell if life still remains.
No faithful companion,
No friend,
No one is left
To answer when I call.

To keep her lips sealed —
That was her old habit.
And I — desperate now
For a single word from her mouth.

The little life that remains in me,
And the untouched, lovely garden of my days,
Have both grown dim and weary
In her long absence —
Silent,
For years unbloomed.

Like a blue lotus beneath a dark cloud,
Her glow — pale as steeped tea,
Fragile as a scarecrow in the storm —
Kills me, moment by moment.

In the crowded mist of night,
The path before me
Is lost in darkness —
No light,
No end in sight.

Her coming — or not coming —
Remained uncertain.
And once I knew that,
What else was left for me to do?
What could I have done?

Somehow, I steadied
This restless, untamed mind —
Held it in my own fragile grasp.
But tell me —
Would anyone, in a broken boat,
Without even a drop of water beneath,
Still wish to cross the river?
Or perhaps,
Each time I recalled
The black mole beneath her lips,
Her absence struck me faint —
Again and again.

What else was left
For me to command or control,
That I could have done —
And failed not to?

Who Are You?

Who are you?
Why have you come here?
Have you come only to torment me
In this final moment,
And steal the breath that still clings to me?

For some forgotten merit of the past,
I have dragged through years
Of a miserable life —
Not dying,
Yet dying each day, each night,
Piece by piece.

Have you come now,
Only to look at me once more —
For the last time?

If you had planned,
Through some cunning or cruelty,
To take away the rest of my life —
You could have come boldly,
Like a merciless assassin,
And struck me with a knife.

If your desire was bound
To some rare, unattainable treasure,
You could have spoken —
And perhaps, you would have had it.

Then why,
For a diseased, decaying body like mine,
For a world already broken and burnt,
Did you toil so hard to come?

I belong nowhere —
Just a wretched soul,
Didn't you already know that?

Today I am here —
Who knows where I'll be tomorrow,
Or if I'll be at all?

Last night, like every other night,
I woke from dreadful dreams,
Gasping, trembling,
And like a stubborn child,
I wept again and again.

But now —
How can I ever open my heart
And cry like that once more?

Before the night ends,
It's been so many days now —
I keep seeing you in my dreams.

And each time you appear,
Your face turns —
Exactly like the face of a devil.

Each time I see you thus,
A nameless terror
Slices through me —
From my feet to my forehead,
I shiver like a severed head,
Awake yet lifeless.

And every time,
In that ocean of dreams,
I find myself
On some distant shore —
Rotting,
Like a forgotten corpse
Washed ashore by time.

Swollen and stinking,
An unclaimed body lies still —
And people, whispering among themselves,
Begin to invent stories.

Once they knew I was unreal — just dust and myth —
They searched no further,
And quietly went their separate ways.

If I am false,
Then tell me — what truth are you,
That you could ever reach out
And touch me?

Each time you raise your hand toward me,
I drift away —
Like a floating cloud, dissolving,
Farther and farther from your grasp.

Once they knew I was asatya,
A name erased from earth —
How could you,
So easily,
Hope to touch me again?

Once the boundary
Of patience and faith is broken,
If you had come
To take my breath away,
Like a blood-faced goddess,
You would have arrived
Draped in silk,
Carved and folded like a sacred relic.

In the soft, pale moonlight
Of the autumn season,
Scented like sandalwood,
I would have slowly faded,
Melting away
Into a lonely, deserted hour —
Whether in season or out of it,
In silence,
In emptiness,
Disappearing like a whispered prayer.

Do as you wish,
My goddess —
Take my body, slice it into flesh,
Claim my patience, my courage, my fiery valor.
Take my shield, my earrings, my desires —
All, without restraint.

If you can,
Bind my entire life's tale
Into the folds of your khanduapatani silk saree —
Every love letter,
Every black-and-white duet photograph,
Every half-written, incomplete poem —
Tie them in knots within its sacred hem.

Do as you will, my goddess —
Take it all.
And yet,
Leave me just a little peace…
Just enough
To die slowly,
With some measure of grace.

Devil

Oh—how late the night has grown,
Why sit here still,
Why not return home?

At such an hour, what noble guest remains to come?
For whom do you wander again and again,
Like a mad soul beneath a sleepless sky?

Your fate and mine—
Already entwined since ages unknown.
For countless lifetimes,
This bond shall remain,
And for that,
We both must suffer the burden of this existence.

Did you not already know this,
My unfortunate one?
What was there left to seek—
When joy and sorrow both
Had long accepted their command from destiny?
No other path was ever open to us.
Again and again,
Changing her adornments, her colors, her form—
Like a Dakini, she lingered beside me,
Through endless nights and weary days.

For thirty-six long years,
In this miserable bed of breath and bones,
We have lain—
Not to taste the pleasures of this birth,
But to repay the debts of lives before.

Then tell me—
How could she gather the will
To step beyond the threshold,
And leave this house of fate behind?

Hope for complete recovery,
Or despair at its absence —
Falling ill,
Back and forth, from home to hospital,
From hospital to home,
How many times have you wandered this path?

And each time you set out,
Like a stubborn bullock,
Halfway through,
You turned back again.

I have met countless gods and goddesses,
Worshipped them not by ritual, but by will.
Tell me — what part of you have I ever denied?
Yet now again,
Leaving behind home, son, daughter-in-law,
Grandchildren and all —
You sit here, plotting to make me alone once more.

Even knowing that the stars,
The time, the constellations —
Are all misaligned,
If still you wish to go — then go.

Go to the monastery you love,
Or a distant temple,
An ashram lost in silence,
Or some unknown kingdom
Where no one has heard our names.

But do not weep before me,
Like a child with trembling lips.
Even if you leave for the rarest of cities,
You will find no peace, no rest —
Not without me.
Do I not know that already?

Yet still,
If you must go —
Then go.

Devil (1)

Speak once, with your heart wide open—tell me,
Why does my name wound you so?
Why this fire of anger at the sound of me?

Is it my past, or a future I will never have,
That you cannot bear?
Is it the ugly guise of a devil —
My face turned blue and strange —
That makes your body tremble,
Shuddering as if struck by cold thunder?

I never wished — not in a single day —
to become your only witness,
to bid you farewell so soon.

Before the destined hour,
I had thought to drown myself in some lake —
but there was no water.

Clutching the rope of a drifting boat,
I sought a resting place,
and instead found only
a forsaken port , fallen and still,
by the lonely edge
of a river without name.

If you must kill me now —
then begin from the beginning.
I have come, after reading
every sign, every star, every shadowed hour,
and stood before you, near yet distant.

All that has passed —
and all that will linger
till the last trembling breath —
who has the time now
to account for it all?

From the fire that marked my birth
to the fire that will claim my death,
for years you guarded me —
a staff in hand,
like a radiant angel
from some unknown star.

Once, I was beside you —
wasn't I?
Yet the moment you glimpsed
the shadowed face within me,
you turned away,
as if the devil himself
had borrowed my form.

Devil (2)

Now — my turn has come.
From beneath the sea,
out of the crystal depths of queen's palace
I will rise —
trembling, gasping, breaking through.

Through three generations of the living and the lost,
I shall pass unseen,
emerging from the forsaken tunnel
of some ancient cave.

And then, like a puppet-master of fate,
I will make you dance —
a fragile plastic doll
in the hands of my fury.

Ask me once — how will I die?
Cast out from home in that eunuch-like ruin of life,
Wandering the nights — have you ever looked at me
even once?

Have you ever held me — and found me slip away,
Choking on the inability to keep you close?
I am dying, moment by moment, in that suffocation.

Have you tried to understand — even once —
That I was born a devil by the fruit of past lives?
What use are wishes then — desires or refusals —
When none of it matters?

No one has the right to look for
a heart already sold to fate.
To lodge under some courtyard in winter's cold —
That was never written in my destiny.

My veins still throb —
fresh blood trembling through a body
of rotting flesh and weary disease.

A lifetime of failures
has earned me nothing but a void —
a blank, green chapter
in the endless history
of merciless repetition.

This destiny — cruel, unbending —
records every moment
my trembling hands reached for someone
and touched only air.

Have you ever tried to understand
that kind of strength —
the breaking strength
that shatters like stone
into soft, helpless wind?

And still — whenever you wished —
you came, again and again,
to strike, to test,
to exhaust what remained
of this old devil's patience.

Breaking free from illusion and desire,
in the twilight of your remaining days,
you return — in the form of a yogini —
throughout the endless night,

striving, searching, circling me,
like a lover from some fabled city,
appearing in every breath, every moment of dream,
tormenting me —
again and again,
with the sweetness of pain.

Once Again, My Beloved

Are you a fragment of the drifting cloud,
half-spread in the dark blue sky of my monsoon dream?
Why do you appear so alluring,
standing between life and death —
a mystery wrapped in mist?

Across endless horizons, I search —
no path, no sign.
Are you a directionless, unknown bird
flying alone, fearless,
untouched by shame,
free of doubt?

In a forest of thorns,
you bloom as my secret garden —
your braid adorned with blue Aparajita,
feet tinted with crimson Alta,
your scent woven with sandalwood and turmeric.
Like a broken cloud at twilight,
you shimmer — beautiful, divine.

Your thoughts — gentle and pure,
your soul — serene and vast.

Once again, my beloved,
after years of distance and silence,
loosen the knot of your hair —
let the harvest of pearls fall freely
from the forest of your deep blue tresses.

Whether you are near or far,
in the pale courtyard of a faded sky,
I spend the whole night
in restless rain,
burning, trembling —
singing tuneless ghazals
to your memory.
Like a drifting fragment of a dark blue cloud,
your memory sometimes floats across my mind —
and disappears into the silence of departure.

Why does it happen so — without reason?
The pain rises again,
and again it spreads —
through the body,
through the bones,
through every trembling joint of being.

All night, the rain breathes through the wind —
across the sky, through the vast ether beyond.
With every rhythm, with every raga,
the divine wings of the clouds dance —
whirling, swaying,
in their celestial procession.

Cloud after cloud flows
through the boundless expanse —
a moving mandala
of storm and song.

I lose control of myself —
suddenly it arrives,
like the season of rain,
like thunder striking the veins.

At the sound of your name,
the sound of clouds begins to beat —
and warmth surges through my blood,
spreading fire through every limb.

Each time your memory returns,
the body burns again —
a fever of love
that knows no cure.

Are you a lonely bird
sitting still, blocking the path —
a stranger of the skies, unseen in the next moment,
your body dissolving into dust,
rolling upon the earth like a fragile clay pot?

In the lap of a cloud-filled sky,
the second god —
this fleeting moment —
dances in divine rhythm.

Begger Woman

Why have you come here
in the guise of a beggar?

What rare treasures
did you leave behind when you departed —
those precious things
you could not carry with you?

Have you returned after all these years
just to reclaim them?

This wretched one
will open the box of memories you left sealed —
and place each forgotten fragment
back into your waiting hands.

After so many years, once again,
you stand before that house —
hands stretched out,
in the form of a beggar.

But tell me — whose house is that?
Everything that looks like a home
is not truly a home.
The rooms may be filled with things,

but they all belong
to the miserable one within.

In your stubborn pride,
you cut away three lines of fate —
and since the day you left,
this house has never been a home.

Crowded with ghosts, false saints,
wandering monks and passing guests,
it has become a house much talked about —
yet stripped of grace,
it rises and falls like a weary shadow.

Since the day you walked away,
nothing has changed —
the house remains just as it was.

The master who once lived here —
is he alive, or long dead?
No one knows.

He drifts through the kingdom
like a man without manhood,
and who among them
keeps count of his silence,
or knows his new address,
his hidden dwelling?

Whom shall I tell
the story of my sorrow?

The people of the village —
they shamed me,
drove me away,
as if I were nothing.

In tattered clothes,
half-naked,
I was chased —
like cattle herded down the road,
their laughter echoing behind me.

They followed, jeered,
until I was gone —
and then,
one by one,
they all returned
to their homes.

Disguised as a beggar,
I went to speak to my own fate —
yet it was myself I kept searching for.

After thirty-six long years,
I only wished
to catch a glimpse
of the beloved man once more.

But not seeing him —
I returned, broken,
drowned in my own misery.

Never, not even in dreams,
had I imagined
such an ending.

Now is the time
to keep living — breath by burning breath,
just to endure the pain.

I belong neither to this shore
nor to the other —
yet this flaming soul
still trembles to see him,
just once more.

Perhaps in this life
I shall never see him again.
Until that moment comes,
I wander —
in the guise of a beggar,
moving silently from place to place,
hiding my tears in dust.

In this beggar's form
I shall roam through
what remains of my life.

Bisakha

Last night, when sleep broke suddenly,
I called out — "Bishakha… Bishakha…"
again and again,
crying in helpless longing.

Each time I spoke your name,
a silent fear,
an unknown terror,
rose within me —

and like a piece of sandalwood
burning from the inside,
I kept turning to ash
within myself.

After sleep shattered,
I could neither rest nor rise.

Through half-closed eyes,
dark glasses masking my gaze,
like an old man of sixty-four,
I wandered — searching, endlessly —
for you, here and there.

You hovered like a dark cloud,
just beyond my reach,
veiled in the vast sky,
as if wanting to be seen, yet unseen,
and I had to turn away
from the yearning in my own hands.

Bishakha… Bishakha…
I called you, over and over,
yet not once did you hear.

The same beloved,
the final love from thirty-six years ago —
did you turn your face, even slightly, to see me?

Like a fresh climber,
wrapped around thorns,
I grew, branch by branch,
year by year,
winding through the alleys near your home.

I was bound
by your love,
lost in its twists and turns.

How could you have forgotten me?

That house, once so renowned,
is no longer a home.

Blinded by loveless love,
I stubbornly linger near you,

yearning for a single kiss
tinged in pale deep blue.

You do not know —
since the day you left,
that house has sat, adorned and waiting,
keeping the weight of responsibility
in its silent gaze.

Beloved

Surangini, speak but once,
and I shall bring you
a blue lotus from the pond.

If even that does not please you,
then from Amarabatipur
I shall gather a hundred thousand parijats
and lay them at your feet,
offering all with love unbound.

With the waters of turmeric,
I shall anoint your sacred limbs.

Mixed with camphor and sandalwood,
in fragrant streams,
I shall adorn your beautiful forehead
like the artistry of a divine muse.
Surangini, not for a day or two —
but for thirty-six long years,
I have shared your joys and sorrows,
stood by your side through it all.

All that I had — whatever little remained —
I gave to you, freely, without reason.

Now, there is nothing left in me to offer.
For whom else could I have kept anything,
if not for you?

Like generous donor Karna of the Mahabharata,
I have given you everything —
my wealth, my heart, my very being.

In fullness and in emptiness,
in bondage and in freedom,
in passion and in renunciation —
I chose you
as my companion for this lifetime.

Beyond death, I shall carry nothing —
save six humble pieces of wood
for my resting pyre,
and a handful of the Ganga's water.

Surangini !
if the measure of my remaining days
could bring peace to your longing,
then come to me quietly —
not as a destroyer,
but as the flame that releases pain.

Touch me
with the strength of all the sacred tongues
your spirit knows,
and let my being dissolve
into your infinite light.

The Season And It's Absence

What is the name of that season, O Gayatri,
where spring never blooms,
yet the crowd swells endlessly?

What is that time, O Gayatri,
where love does not arise,
yet the clay of the body burns in longing,
silently, within itself?

There exists such a season upon this mortal earth, O Gayatri—
where union is absent, yet renunciation breathes;
where hope has withered,
yet the dust of despair stretches for miles;
where union and separation,
like the serpents of Rahu,
devour the remaining breaths of life.

Tell me, Gayatri, what is the name of this strange season?
Like an unknown guest, it arrives uninvited,
shows its face for a fleeting moment—
then turns back midway, vanishing into silence.
Once it departs,
no vision of it is ever seen again.
Is that season the strange echo
of nestless birds—

a time of little sparrows crying in the wind?
Or is it the season
of a newly widowed heart, trembling in its ache?

Is it the season steeped
in the memories of those
who live with unspoken inability—
a nectar distilled from silent suffering?

Do you know, Gayatri,
its face, its color, its splendor?
Have you ever seen
the shape of its sorrow?

What flower blooms in that season, Gayatri?
Is it a half-born season,
a fragment of time that never completes itself?

Is it the season when rainclouds
rumble over the ripened millet fields—
a song of restless thunder?

Or is it the season of the first beloved,
draped in a silk sari of Nile-blue,
an apsara descending from memory?

Or perhaps, Gayatri—
is it the crimson seasonless time
of a bride grown silent with years,
her vermilion fading into dusk?

If you know,
tell me, Gayatri.

In Thirteen Days

An untimely guest — gone within thirteen days,
How many promises scattered on my doorway's haze.
I pleaded, I reasoned — but she wouldn't hear,
With stubborn grace she crossed the gate, so clear.
Once gone, she never turned around —
No backward glance, no echo, no sound.

After she left,
The house felt haunted —
As if its hollow walls whispered her sound,
And fell upon me, heavy and cold.
My feet slipped,
Dangling from the last step
Of a dark, endless tunnel —
Half in shadow, half in memory.

And watching, watching — thirty-six years have passed.
In the smoke of bullets and fireworks' cruel play,
Amid bombings and blockades,
And the chants of restless strikes —
So many bloodstains marked the roads,
So many familiar faces
Faded from the frame of vision.
Who has the time

To keep count of all that's lost?
Carrying the weight of past births within,
I have grown old —
Inside this unending moment.

Behind these thirty-six years
stands that five-foot-seven, emaciated boy —
no longer a tongue of rebellion,
but a fading echo of it.
His white, unkempt hair,
once light as drifting petals,
now dyed to hide the passing wind of time.
Weighing this mortal frame,
clutching a beggar's bowl like a monk,
I wander here —
a restless yogi,
troubled by the silence of his own becoming.

They said — Aries bears the curse of Kalsarp Yog,
Anuradha, did you not know?
Ignoring every warning,
You counted the days — one by one —
And on the thirteenth, you left home.

In your absence,
I stand between two distant shores,
Waters rising endlessly around me.
Did you not think — even once —
How I would cross this flood alone?

Anuradha, after you left,
This crystal home feels like a dense forest —

Silent, shadowed, and lost in itself.
Yet somewhere, someday,
Our paths will meet again —
I live within that hope

Madness

Take me away, O beloved of my madness—
That stubborn dreamer from the dusky forest of falsehoods,
From the blind lanes of desire's decay,
From the uncertain valley of death's delay—
Draw me into the warmth of your lap,
And ferry me beyond this birth's weary shore.

O my reckless, unrepentant love!
Hold my hand and lead me to a realm
Where geography has no history,
Where no home nor beginning exists—
Where, in the dawn of a grand celestial celebration,
The fragrance of blooming Brahma-kamal
Will send shivers of peace through this mortal frame.

Let them understand—or not.
I know, my love, like unfinished time itself,
You are my first and final devotion.
If you must take me, take all that I am—
And like a blind honeybee, trembling in its last breath,
Let me hum your name till the end of time.
Like an untamed yogini sipping from the chalice of love,
I burn in the forest of longing—
Each day consumed in the fire of separation.

My body, like a brittle reed,
Breaks again and again in the temple of my own mind.

In the twilight of ruin, like an ancient, dying tree,
As I fall into dust, I see—
Your radiant face flashing before my eyes,
Shimmering like the light of moonlit
At the hour of cosmic dissolution.

How long have I lived confined within my own borders,
Clinging to the sweet illusion
That one day you will arrive—
At the very center of my sacred circle.
And before my final breath escapes,
Let me whisper once more—
Love me… love me,
As I have loved you through countless
Births and endless time.

Whether in this lifetime or not—
Is that truly sorrow?
For through countless births and endless aeons,
We shall remain bound—two souls, one thread.

Until the barren fields of our fate
Bloom again with tender green,
We shall stay entwined—
Unbroken, unforgotten,
In the silent rhythm of forever.

In This Midnight Hour

At this late hour—
Who is it knocking upon my bedroom door,
Out of time, out of reason?
Do they not know—I belong to this house only for tonight?
Tomorrow, who can say
If this body and mind will still exist
Here—or anywhere at all?

And last night—who stood there,
Knocking softly, endlessly,
Weeping like a madwoman in the dark,
When not a word was spoken?
The air itself was still—
No crow, no cuckoo, not even a whisper.
Only that strange sound of sorrow,
As if the silence had learned to cry,
And the night, unable to bear it,
Held its breath till dawn.

If you look at me that way,
I've been fearful and shy since childhood.
I never learned to speak another's pain—
Every feeling, every word,
Rises first to my eyes before my lips can say a thing.

With great pain I held myself still—
In half-sleeping eyes,
I lay quiet upon that wooden bed,
Face turned toward the north.

In the darkened house, lost in its black corridors,
I rose, startled by fear,
And opened the door—
Looked inside, looked out,
Searched every corner of the night—
But she was nowhere.

Not finding her, not speaking a word,
I turned back slowly,
And returned to my silence once again.

When the lids of my eyes begin to fall,
That devil's form—like a painted woman—
Flickers before my sight.

As though in the autumn sky,
A cloud, dark yet gleaming with joy,
Promises to rain with thunder's voice—
Yet holds itself back,
Hovering on the edge of becoming.

Unable to break free from bonds,
From the weight of worldly life,
I writhed in sleepless nights,
Haunted by thoughts of a future
As uncertain as a caged bird's sky.

Blaming no one else,
I turned my anger inward—
Cursing my own fate,
And my ignorance that chained me
To this endless circle of return.

While Leaving Home

As I stepped out, all ready to depart,
the first face I saw before my eyes—
was not the same as thirty-six years apart.

Shapes have shifted, colours changed,
so many faces, once close, once dear,
have faded from the map of my mind,
like stars erased by morning's tear.

I never kept their count, nor tried—
they vanished quietly, side by side.

Like a still frame from a sorrowed noon,
that face remained—a silent tune.
I know not what I felt that day,
but all my life, in some quiet way,
for that one face—
I've kept dying, bit by bit, each day.

On the road I took to leave,
whoever I met along the way—
I could not pause,
not even for a moment.

Why would I stop?
Who were they to me?

The needless burden of my breath?
Fellow travelers of feeling and its absence?
Cunning comrades of inhumanity—
or perhaps,
the madness born of my own failures?

But keeping faith as my witness,
I had vowed—
never to meet that one again in this life;
and even if we crossed paths,
I would turn away,
walk another road.
Yet tell me—
did I keep my word
till the very end?

So beautiful was your face—
like the idol of Lakshmi herself,
adorned with a garland
of a thousand blue Aparajita flowers.

Your body—like a damp celestial nymph,
bathing in the deep green heart
of some unreachable constellation;

Your hair—silent as a forest maiden's,
mystic, fragrant, still.

And after the passing of just one season,
I found myself
fallen in love with her.

Are you doing well?
How do you pass such long, silent days?
Do my words ever cross your mind?

Even when I longed to ask
such meaningless questions,
I stayed quiet—
because I had already given myself
the answers
to every question that could be asked.

Wrapped in a mist-coloured drape,
she stood there—
her body veiled in the dim hue of fog.

Suddenly she turned,
stepping before me,
blocking my path.

In a trembling voice,
a voice I could barely hear, she said—
"You're still the same
as you were thirty-six years ago.
How much longer will you punish me?
This unfortunate life refuses to end.
Can't you see?
I lie here, mingled with the dust itself—
when will you ever understand that?"

Without saying a word,
like a miserable, broken soul,
I walked ahead—

the road rising and falling beneath my feet,
like waves in a restless sea.

Till that beautiful woman
faded into the unseen,
I forgot my own being,
and drifted—
floating in a dream.

The Passionate Lover

With a half-bloomed jasmine tied softly to his hand,
He came — like a stranger straying
from some forgotten tree,
a passionate wanderer entering my well-known home.

He came, yes — and I am glad he did,
but without a word, without a sign,
he let the night slip away in silence—
and by dawn,
my once-secure world lay
In ruins of its own fragrance.

Like the guardian of this world and the next,
if his coming here was fated,
then why, after years of distance,
did he claim a one-sided right—
as though I were still his own reflection?

If time itself kept us apart for ages,
how did he find the courage
to declare ownership
over what love had already set free?

On a crumpled bed, through years of slow dying,
lived the cursed one —
a shadow pressed against the southern wall of time.

He — just a name now, a lifeless photograph,
his face blurred by fog, unreachable,
like a faint line of light floating
from some unseen valley afar.

Absent, yet near —
in every heartbeat, in every breath,
his nearness feels like distance reborn.

Like a Bhubanomohini — an enchantress divine —
the smile on that radiant beauty's lips
was all that remained for my mortal life to lose.

But tell me —
did that unknowing lover ever realize
how little of me was left to surrender?

He came — that proud, intoxicated lover —
since the day his foot crossed my threshold,
the house has known no rest.

Relatives near and far,
in time and out of time,
kept gathering like whispers of old dust—
and one by one, like shadows of Chaitali,
they slipped away into their own forgotten paths.

And he — after thirty-six long years,
has he come to dig up
the wounds time had tried to bury?
Has he returned
to take revenge
on the quiet I had learned to live within.

From the moment his lotus flower
touched the threshold of this cursed home,
it ceased to be a home at all.

For years, we lived through the echoes
of small, forgotten incidents —
not conversations, but after-conversations,
bitter murmurs of what should have stayed unsaid.

Between our being and not-being,
no difference remained—
only the faint scent of something once sacred,
now fading into dust.

The Sacred Boundary

Beyond that sacred boundary of Lakshman's rekha
lies your tiny, beautiful village—
so small, yet large enough to hold my whole ache.

Once, secretly, I wished to go there—
to slip away like an escapist
into the hush of your lanes.
But how could I?

For years I've been rolling here,
like a mad soul caged in her own dust.
No handful of earth beneath my feet,
no ground to claim as mine—
only the illusion of two feet
that never learned to arrive.

And each time I dressed,
ready to come to you,
some urgent errand of fate
dragged me back halfway home.

Your village lies so close, so lovely—
and yet, I feel you are far,
as distant as a dream wrapped in mist.

Even if your Labanyamayee village
exists only in memory today,
someday—yes, someday—
I will cross that Lakshman Rekha
and come to you.

But will I truly make it there?
For as long as I live half-lived,
like a broken idol left on its side,
I remain here—
on this crumpled bed, beneath this weary sheet.

After years of lying still,
who really remains in control of their own body?

This ancient frame, this tired mind—
they are no longer bound
by will or unwill, by joy or sorrow,
as silk once bound the living flesh.

Before another hand dares to reach you,
I will go—
I will reach you first.

Across the seven seas and thirteen rivers,
beneath the depths of water,
there must lie a palace—
and within it, a chest,
where you are held captive by some unseen devil.

I will free you from him—
tear open that dark vault and bring you back.
But tell me—how will I?

Now I wander like a fallen yogi,
a begging bowl in my hands,
moving from door to door,
stripped of youth,
drained of strength,
left only with memory and prayer.

Yet still, I vow—
if I could but lift you once more from that realm,
I would return to this mortal world
crowned not with gold,
but with the glory of having reached you.

This dust-laden house,
like a heap of discarded relics,
has lain lonely since the day you left.

Its doors and windows never open—
yet the Sun and Moon
enter freely, uninvited.

Clutching my fate, I remain here,
bound to karma,
marking each passing day
with a cross in my secret diary—
twenty-four hours of silence,
written in invisible pain.

My ailing body, fragile as breath,
slowly tears itself away
from the web of affection and illusion.

And I whisper to myself—
the cement must be slipping away,
the walls decaying,
where hangs that broken mirror—
mercuryless,
reflecting nothing
but the ruin of its own light.

How could I ever find the courage
to go to your village at a single moment?

A lovely lady like you,
sitting there, in that village,
waiting for someone—
who knows whose heart she holds in hope?

The memories of our first love—
they will not allow this unfortunate soul
to simply come and meet you,
not without the weight of time
and the quiet agony of the past.

In the illustrated geography of memory,
your village will always remain
etched on my heart.

Could I ever forget that place?
No—I will never set foot in your village
without crossing the sacred Lakshman Rekha.

Whether I step across or not,
I will tell you—
at the right time,
without fail.

Will Go, But!

Saying, "I will go, I will go,"
with my feet ready to leave—
since when have I been sitting
in this very house?

Over this house,
I no longer have any authority as before.

Nor, like any human being,
am I counted
in this house anymore.

Without knowing the difference
between yesterday and wisdom,
I now sit here—
only in name,
like a security guard,
watching it.

A house without windows or doors
cannot be counted as a home.

And for her—
I am not longing anymore.

In this vast, dark night,
like the cries of ghosts and spirits,
the teak wood bed creaks—
and leaping from its ancient frame,
he breaks away from his beautiful wife,
casting off every thread of affection and illusion.

Even after answering
every question justly,
and comforting my beloved,
he bends into the grand festival of colors—
lost in the scent and spell
of countless hibiscus blooms—
and leaves, one-sided and unlooking.

But I—
I cannot go.

Each time I have dressed and set out to leave,
my beautiful wife—
like a shadow—has traced my path,
sitting silently in wait.

Each time, facing north,
adorned with tilak and sandal,
wearing the Tulsi beads
like a living statue,
she looks at me—
and the image of my mother left behind
drives me to madness.

In the illusion of this rare home,

I rise and fall like a stubborn ox.
How many times have I wondered—
is this house truly mine?

My being or not-being
makes no difference here,
for a court still runs there
over countless snakes, kites, devils, and ghosts.

Half-built, half-broken,
strung together in a garland of words
whose meanings I cannot grasp,
day and night chattering endlessly
are my two sons—Rahul and Rohan.

Like a half-placed, faithful security guard,
I have been watching that ancient house.

No matter how much I long,
no matter how suffocated I feel,
I cannot step beyond the threshold—
this house will not let me go.

The Hope Of Baitarani

Gori, oh Gori,
Gori, oh Gori…

I am dying in your longing,
and you—pierce me with every word,
turning my wounds into a slow death of life.

Your laughter smells of attar,
and my youth lies wasted,
scorched beneath the fire of desire.

Your turmeric-hued face
has gone to the pyre of death,
and with your veil draped gently over it,
I will hold you—carefully,
with every ounce of my striving.

Gori, oh Gori,
Gori, oh Gori…

If you touch me, you will melt away;
if I touch you, I will be undone.

Do not touch me,
and I will not touch you.

In just two days of meeting,
how much of each of us is spent?

Dreaming not of lies,
we search for each other
within the fragile realm of our dreams.

Gori, oh Gori,
Gori, oh Gori…

The thread of love has snapped.
In just two days of meeting,
you opened your chest,
and I opened my heart.

Waves stir in your mind—
empty, drifting dreams
float endlessly,
and in my heart,
storm after storm
rises, untimely and unbidden.

Gori, oh Gori,
Gori, oh Gori…

Why have you made me suffer so?
Kohl in your eyes,
the red of Holi on your lips.

Where is your home? What is your name?
You have said nothing—
you have spoken nothing.

In these two days of the world,
nothing remained,
and nothing will remain.

When Will You Return

Since when have you gone?
I remember neither the day, nor the date.
Since when have you gone—
gone, and never looked back.

Not a single letter you wrote.
Tell me, truly—
is it time that's lacking,
or heart?

How long has it been since you left?
That boundary I drew last spring—
I still haven't crossed it.

The flowers that bloomed in your courtyard,
their fragrance I search for here,
but cannot find.

How long has it been since you left?
In annoyance, in ache, in weary silence,
I light a torch of memory inside this house
and warm myself by its fire.

In the sky of your mind,
my kites still flutter—

and I keep pulling, pulling
at their invisible threads.

You left—
and once gone, you never returned.
You wrote nothing—
neither good nor bad.

How are your days passing now?
Here in Puri,
my life grows desperate—
splintered by hatred, jealousy, irritation.

With your own hands,
you are breaking
the very forest of flowers
you once planted.

In restless yearning,
I keep counting the days.

Memory

From the factory's chimney,
black smoke rises to the sky.
In the land of Kaunri Kamakhya,
a strange alchemy awakens.

In village, brimming with strange alchemy,
in the narrow lanes of the settlement
echo obscene cries.

Among the mob of street boys,
a burning house—
and in the blur of forgetfulness,
every scene
slowly fades,
turning invisible.

Oh beautiful, I am the emperor of your dreams—
lost in a silver basket
filled with the stars of the sky.

With tired, longing eyes
I keep searching, endlessly,
for a way out—
at a lonely, three-cornered crossroads
where silence itself seems to wait.

In your breath, my blood ignites—
like the flame of a trembling lamp.

In the fragrance of my nerves,
your body begins to shiver.

Though within reasonless silence,
and unspoken conception,
your lips still offer
a secret kiss.

In some silent gesture,
in a fleeting glance so magnetic,
you surrendered yourself.

Your gathered youth—
a treasure of lifetimes—
is the rarest jewel
this life could ever hold.

Oh beautiful one,
do not set fire to my blood.

You are my river,
my constellation, my woman—
you are the pilgrim
of my deepest memories.

Canvas

You were to come—
why did you not?
Counting stars,
the night quietly dissolved.
On the river of life,
we stand on two silent shores.
Hope has fallen apart,
and patience—
no longer remains.

In sky after sky,
unseasonal storms arise;
deep within the mind,
desires gather like crowds.
You did not come—
I keep counting the days,
turning half-mad,
for even the night
refuses to end.

The lamp's flame flickers,
trembling as it burns.
In tuneless notes,
I draw uncertain lines,
waiting for your return.

From the breaking of sleep
to the pale light of dawn,
I listen closely—
to that unforgettable tune,
filled with such aching emotion.

All is silent—
color fades in the sky,
love fades in the heart.
Tasteless, scentless,
the lamp's flame flickers alone.
Sitting in solitude,
I keep drawing—
your outline.

A shelf filled with memories,
in the trunk of my mind,
carefully, secretly kept.
You would never understand
how miserable a poet's life can be—
in dreams, in dreams,
he keeps wandering, restless.

Come, or do not come—
on tiptoe,
in the hush of early dawn,
I sit alone,
tracing, with quiet devotion,
the outline of you.

Meloncholy

Nothing feels right—
the melancholy wind drifts,
like a broken kite
bowed low,
lost in its own flight.
Above, on the electric wire,
the street lies empty,
no vehicle stirring its quiet.
A lone figure stands,
iron rod clutched in both hands,
eyes lifted to the open sky.

Is your body trembling
in the chill of the wind?
How many more nights
until I can hold you
and show you the stars?
From the sea of blood I rise,
dancing, alive,
for the red sun—
a new child is coming.
I will bring
new garments,
soft and bright,
to welcome
this new life.

Nothing feels right—
the time to call has passed,
yet my restlessness does not grow.
Still, I am certain
that you will sweep away
my melancholy thoughts,
and speak royal tales.
And like a fool,
I will fly kites
over the rooftops of our home

Set No Terms

Until the unknown tomorrow,
envelop me
with the life of your sins and virtues.
Place no conditions—
let it be absolute,
free, and complete.

Adorn my pride and arrogance
with gentle care,
and keep them safe
in the shimmer of your blue veil.
Without hesitation,
place no conditions,
let it all be free.

O Earthly embodiment
Of countless imaginations,
my Goddess,
look upon me once
with your tender gaze.
See how, in shyness, I hide my face—
like the lustful Sun in Ahalya's cottage,
how my body, soaked in blood,
is being healed by the lake of Byasa,
in the great forest of regret.

What a distant, unreachable feeling—
neither do the flowers fall,
nor do the leaves stir.

Time itself has frozen
in a meditative pose.
The sky above lies still,
the earth beneath heavy with sorrow,
and in the wind of the heavens,
like a weary bumblebee,
my life's fragile leaf
is shattered in grief.

In a pious hour,
he sits and paints—
a cunning artist, born of inauspicious time.

With brush and color,
he brings to life
the slow, fierce morning of blue,
a morning spun
from countless imaginings.

Without you, this festival
is a silent, meaningless night.
Our love
remains eternally unblemished
on this painted, vibrant earth.

Devi

Rise, children, rise in the courtyard,
the broken house blooms anew,
its scattered curtains swaying
to the ghazal of drifting clouds.
On the widow's brow tonight,
the tender rites of the enchanted night glimmer,
and in Hirakpur's soft, golden light,
the stars play, dripping silver joy.
Among the children, in the courtyard,
the shattered home awakens,
singing softly—alive again
with laughter, life, and light.

Rise now, in the morning light,
to leave behind a past
overflowing with dreams.

At ten o'clock, the office calls,
life bound in routine,
where ideals are paraded,
and authority wears its mask.
Forget the past,
rich with whispered dreams,
and step gently
into the unknown tomorrow.

Rise, within the green envelope of infertile clouds,
the Sun writes beautiful letters
in golden ink.

In her polished green hair,
a garland is being tied—
the spinster,
while in supreme detachment,
the powerless minister
rolls the rudraksha mala.

Amid the gunshots of the mafia,
shivering shells lie on the deep-blue carpet.
In the frozen dance of passion,
the struggle rages for the belly,
while the dead crabs demand their strike.

And yet,
independence is being orchestrated,
in all its strange, relentless form.

Rise, awaken, and come,
from the timeless fortress of countless dreams,
borne on the wandering wind.
The tremor of intimate passion shivers,
the seasonal breeze drifts,
heavy with honeyed fragrance,
and the devoted surrender
of the Baitarani's tides.
So many events begin to stir,
unfolding slowly,
at the very navel of the forsaken Earth.

Even in your absence,
it feels as if you are present
in every fleeting moment—

like clouds heavy with rain,
in the monsoon melodies of Malhar,
in labor,
in meditation,
in the rise and fall of breath,
in the gesture of fearlessness,
in the intoxication of spirit,
in wisdom and effort.

Your arrival
is a welcome,
in the honeyed, moonlit hour of night,
where the sole intoxication
is the memory of your touch.

Rise, the night of devotion is ending swiftly,
come, O devi! come, in this auspicious hour.

In the memory of you,
my body and mind are enchanted,
in the honeyed sweetness
of this radiant night.

54. Solitary in the Emerald Woods

The season of torrential rain sits adorned,
like a young maiden ripened into grace,
resting upon the crown of the sky.

You — near, yet not here —
your absence breathes beside me.

In the cold wind, the body trembles,
goosebumps bloom swiftly upon my skin,
as the chill's soft wings flutter,
by the side of a lonely river.

By the riverside at dusk,
your face flickers faintly in the mirror of memory.
Amid the gathering of trembling stars,
the jasmine garland of night unravels,
tumbling through the green forest —
as the wind, once trapped, bursts free,
and everything sways in its wild release.

In the rhythm of cosmic drum's beat,
the yearning soul begins to tremble sweet —
within the river's quivering stream,
the golden wind unfolds its dream.

Through that breeze, a window sighs,
of memory that wakes and dies —
it opens wide, then softly closes,
bathed in tears and rain-wet roses.

Your shadow, washed in monsoon's grace,
dances through the emerald space —
to the lilting tune the raindrops play,
in the forest's heart at end of day.

I'm trembling with fear, all alone I stand,
in the lonely green forest's silent land.

Alaka Sanyal

You are my moon-blanched fervour,
my Alaka Sanyal.
I dream of you in tender sleep,
in dusky, trembling light.

You appeared suddenly—
bright gossip, quiet nods.
Sachi Babu met you
in Videha's regal splendour,
at Barunavanta,
gathered from the gandharva Chitraratha,
and secured your essence
in the abandoned temple of Nalanda.

Years later, Guru Mohanty found you again,
after relentless search.
You button your blouse,
whisper shyly like a touch-me-not,
and seal yourself gently
in the chair nearby.
You flutter like artful pigeons,
flinging your lusty youth upon the couch,
make love like bashful girls,
become pregnant with desire,
then vanish—
a fleeting constellation.

Your quivering voice takes form
in the squawk of bats or crows;
your absence engulfs Mission Road,
the traders' slums at Jajpur.
Insolent Spring carries your corpse
in a broken, crude stretcher.
You are the moon-blanched passion
of my love, my Alaka Sanyal.

Miles of jungle anguish lie
stretched before my eyes.
Our first meeting: the Tribal Fairground;
second: a solitary cave at Khandagiri.
Countless meetings, worships, horoscopes,
letters in blue envelopes,
endless waitings
on the sizzling sands of time.

For four years, I treasured you
in a closed chamber,
writing your name on blank sheets,
hung round my neck.
That day you longed to move naked,
to soar in the blue sky like a kite,
over Kalinga, the Cardamom shipyards,
or float like a canoe
through New Delhi, Kolkata, Goa,
or some unknown crossroads
of some unknown place.

I could not attain you,
nor could anyone else.

I cannot find you in streets or drains,
the Alka Store or Banaras sweet stall,
Granthalaya bookstore,
morning town buses,
in friends' company or Philosophy class.

You are my dark-haired princess,
the fossil of my love,
my guiding polestar,
the sentinel of relationship.
The raining night roars solitary
on the walls of my house,
reverberating with your voice.

You are my Anima Bastia,
my Alok Meher.
My couch resonates with whispers
craving for you.
I wander this city,
a forlorn ambulant.

May you grow with age,
conquer death,
become perpetual, immortal.
May countless desperate souls
take birth from the womb of the earth,
singing carols of your laurels.

Your Graceful Body

Your body—
oh, your body! In white saree, black saree,
red or green, it all suits you so well.

Upon your form, the spring wind lingers,
Plumeria blooms, Jasmine unfolds,
flowers upon flowers awaken.

Who could stand before you
in this city of desire?

Your body—
especially the map of your form—
I trace the rivers, the keys, the lands within your
streams.

Like a sheep lost along hidden paths,
I am led astray in your maze.
Are you a woman,
or an angel sent from heaven?

In the branches of your hair,
Swati and Arundhati sway like gentle birds,
and we, mere humble wanderers,
drift quietly in the tender dark of your shadow.
Your body—

a sacred pilgrimage where
the infant of my desire wanders untamed,
bathing in the waters of Ganga.

Truly, your form is an untouched island,
where the merchant of my sorrow
places his hands upon my skull,
seeking the bloom of love.

You are the central point of my life,
my ever-flowing, ever-fruiting spring.

I swear it, Golden Girl!
Your yellow, brass-hued body
spins in my mind like a restless wheel—

where hatred, envy, doubt,
and the fear of curses roar
like a herd of startled deer.

And I—just an empty man—
why would you light, for me,
the torch of memory
in this deepening dark?

Your body—
gleaming like the moon
Of full moon night,
your body—
carrying the fragrance of a hundred thousand roses,
blooms gently
in the secret garden of my heart.

Body

In the holy temple of her yearning,
I stand—a simple flute,
a priest, a devotee.

Water drips over the lingam,
and the wind moves like a strange fever,
haunting the shadows
with whispers too secret to name.

In the Konark of her body,
I am a mighty emperor;
yet in the dark night,
I take the role of Dushasana in violation.

From head to toe,
millions of lotus blossoms seem to bloom,
and in the wind,
desperate, miserable memories
stir both body and soul.

The bard of the body's fire,
bearing witness to formless love's desire.

The First Evidence

In the half-night of the suds, I dance,
at the mid hour.
Millions of sparks bloom like blue lightning,
and chanting the great mantra of life,
I am but a humble ascetic.
In the deep of night,
where in the realm of dreams
is the Mansi of my heart?

How small is my domain, how swiftly my years fade,
how much remains in this fleeting fragment of a moment?
Who truly knows the beginning or end
of time's relentless flow?

At this hour, the storm sways like a courtesan in trance,
and in the garden of my mind, forty-nine winds descend in dance.
The storm's trembling wings unfold upon my sight,
their vision flickers—fevered, bright.
Beneath the courtyard of that house long gone,
old memories rise, one by one.
Like a mad poet, I set my blood aflame,
calling rebellion by its forgotten name.
With the trumpet of life's last breath I roam,

seeking my history, my lost spring's home—
the vanished borders of my fading land,
or some small island
where memory still stands.

Who came in that first spring,
sowing seeds and leaving me undone?
Who cast their spell upon my heart,
who taught me the mantra of love?
Why, in my first youth, did you strip me bare—
filling my eyes with intoxication,
and stealing all that I was?
The storm's hanging wings shattered my chariot,
tore my living flesh to pieces,
scattering them across distant towns,
fields, forests, and darkened lanes.

You broke my strength, my pride, my faith—
and the last tender thread of my humanity.

Like an untimely storm, you drifted away one day,
like city boys who let their kites loose in careless play.

You forgot every word, every vow once true,
and left me drowning in sorrow's hue.
My wisdom is lost, my sight grown blind—
no path remains for my trembling mind.
You sailed on a vessel of clouds and mist,
to the moon's pale land where dreams persist,
burning the parade of beauty's flame,
and bartering the body in love's own name.
Now only lightning's silver gleam remains,

and stars that weep through endless rains—
while I, so helpless, drift afar,
searching in vain for who we are.

You left me shattered on life's mid-stairs,
and flung me, burning, into hate's own lair.
You broke my nights, my tender dreams,
and vanished softly—without a gleam.

Now village voices murmur and sting,
their words like arrows whispering.
Who was right, who went astray—
their echoes haunt my every day.
My life lies dim, my heart unsure,
I search myself, but find no cure—
as though my soul has slipped apart,
a stranger now within my heart.

Who took away my fire, my strength, my very might?
I've fallen like a clay doll—
drained, powerless, undone.
All that I'd placed within your hands,
you turned away, refused,
and walked your chosen road.
Yet here I stand,
singing your praise still—
your name, the only echo left in me.

Your joy brings no ache to my heart,
your forgetting me tears no part.
Hate me, envy me, curse my name,
wear the crown of shameful flame—

and wipe away my every sign,
as if I'd never crossed your line.
Though I had no right to speak your name,
I still had hope—a fragile flame.
The hues of my heart have drained away,
love's old intoxication gone astray.
I once thought you a goddess divine,
my worship, my faith, my sacred sign—
but like a corpse that burns in fire,
you twist and fade in love's pyre.
Now I forget you, as all must do,
and you, from this day, forget me too—
as proof of love turns into smoke,
and ashes whisper where passion broke.

Sheltered In Safety

When you are near, I feel safe—
when you leave,
suddenly, fear begins to bloom.

All night—
restlessness, pride,
and quiet weeping.

So many endless words,
so many meanings lost—

my trembling soul swings upon their sound,
stringing word to word in vain,
while you pretend, so easily,
that your pride still remains.

How many truths, how many make-believes entwine—
the broken bond of two entwined worlds.
Lies, words, curses, anger, mistakes—
all gather and fade,
a living death,
crumbling grain by grain.

In the great sacrifice of life, you became mine—
the final offering, the last sacred flame.

Pressed and faded, I remain behind you,
like a shadow clinging to its source,
while all around,
the world collapses into ruin.
Suddenly, the dark night arrives—
you drift away like a plucked flower,
riding the chariot of the storm.
Like a wingless Jatayu,
I fight face to face,
battle after endless battle,
wrestling with the march of time.

You are, yet you are not—
and I stand alone.
Around me, broken things shatter with force—
this miserable, fragile body,
and lines of poetry
that mean nothing anymore.

A seasonal storm rages,
winds fierce on every side.
Silent, in this rented room,
my heart flutters,
beating to the shimmer of restless feet.

You are, yet you are not—
the earth lies silent on every side.
Singing the song of the storm,
alone, so alone,
a dead poet dreams again.

So safe is this home of mine—
made my own, my little nest divine.
And here I sit, listening still,
to your drenched, trembling voice in the wind's chill.

After So Many Years

After so many years, you came in my dream,
at dawn's soft hour, through half-closed eyes' gleam.
In the courtyard of breath, a lingering melody sighs,
its sorrow woven in despair's quiet ties.
And you return—reluctant, unsure.

After many years, you returned in my dream,
your shadow floating in time's gentle stream.
Your smile, a marble statue's quiet grace,
your eyes, pearls shining in their space.
You are the glow of my golden reverie,
My living God, my soul's eternity.

I paint your image—
with countless hues the heart bestows.
With words for brushes,
I craft you, shatter you,
again and again—
between yearning and surrender.

In the quiet will of my soul,
I set afloat a boat of poems;
and as it drifts through your dreams,
I lose myself—
my destiny, my dawn, my name.

Truly, this dawn—
if you do not arrive,
what meaning shall linger
in this fragile glow, this drowsy hush of light?

Between sorrow and silent pride,
I'll pour myself empty,
and drift alone,
through the deep forest,
where even shadows remember your name.

At the quiet end of countless dreams,
I listen intently
to the echo of your word.
I breathe the rhythm of your being—
we are indivisible now,
our love the final essence,
the distilled breath of our souls.

I have dreamt so many dreams—
visions fierce and vast,
where terror takes shape
and the night outgrows itself.

In that dream,
a cry—raw, unending—
splits the void,
trees rise, roots to the sky,
their branches turned to prayer.

A sorcerer commands a bodiless soul to dance,
and though no water dwells within the lake,

a thousand lotuses bloom—
unreasoned, unreal,
yet achingly alive.

In that dream,
my hand snaps like a slender twig,
the mountain of patience shatters suddenly,
and wisdom arrives—aged, uninvited.

Terror bends the spine of faith,
and upon my eyes,
a veil of paralysis falls—
cold, unmoving,
like the silence after a storm of gods.

I call to you aloud—without restraint,
in the helpless hush of dream.
I speak with you there,
not in words,
but through the soft currents
of my subconscious mind,
half-asleep,
half-lost in the tender blur of night.

In your dream,
I lose myself—
forgetting my own being,
like a devoted pilgrim before a broken shrine.
Day and night I sing,
unaware of time's passing,
the eternal song of love—
my only prayer,
my only breath.

You are my final dream—
after countless years,
you will return to me in sleep.
You are the resonance
that fills my every word,
the sound that circles all directions.

Amid sorrow, silence, and weary suffering,
you will come—
in the twilight
of my life's last evening.

Termite Beneath The Tree

Oh, Termite! Beneath the tree, a Kashmiri beauty—
a long-armed shawl draped gracefully over her brow,
a crimson throat, a tilted nose,
like the rider of a galloping steed in royal formation,
leaping from mountain to mountain,
through storms of snow and ice.

Smoke drifts across the sky,
dark clouds entwine the forest.
Amid the wondrous sights,
her beauty gestures in ways beyond words.

The tone of connection shifts,
as life moves in its own rhythm.
In a touch of gentle care,
the meaningless night quietly fades away.

I know not her name,
nor the village where her story begins,
nor the measure of her years.

I fill my eyes with her presence,
letting words stumble and falter,
strange and trembling,
trying to reach her soul.
On the wings of clouds,

the ship of dreams drifts—
and there she is,
unknown yet luminous,
a blush upon her lips,
a fleeting, gentle smile
that lingers like morning light.

My being dissolves,
lost among the mountains of caverned stone.
I am here, yet I am not—
held within the embrace of her beauty.

In my own ignorance, sometimes
I reproach myself,
and speak to myself in quiet despair,
cradled in the lap of dark clouds.

Without oneself, who truly is one's own—
in this prisoned life,
in a rented room,
in a foreign land?

Without oneself, who remains?
In one's own ignorance,
in one's own grief—
who is near, who belongs?

When I gaze upon myself
in moments of solitude,
a strange intimacy stirs—
I become my own companion,
my own wife and son,
and even my condemned God.

Queen

In the blurred murmurs of a miserable soul,
Ranihanspur hums beneath forgotten moons—
Silent Indraprastha sleeps,
Its pearl-palace crumbled into memory's dust.

In the sapphire womb of the Yamuna,
Time's painter still dissolves his brush,
Sketching the sigh of an age undone.
Witness, O Eternal One—
Mahākāl, mute consort of decay,
Guardian of centuries drowned in death.

In veins, memory flows—red and restless,
A ship adrift in the directionless sea
of endless ache.

In vanished gems lie engraved—
Bathing chambers, courts of colour,
secret inner rooms,
and the fading portrait
of a queen who still dreams
inside the dust of her ruin.

The throne lies empty,
the court—grey, discoloured, dim.

An ominous omen whirls
in circular silence,
while Time itself
stands markless—
without beginning,
without end.

In the fierce outcry of a crucified soul,
the royal hall trembles—
The palace of colours quakes,
as from the proud breasts
of a lust-drunk dancer
falls her silken veil—
and through the living world
echoes the hiss of fear,
wrapping creation
in its shivering breath.

The dead soul of the queen
beckons me with a sign—
But I am but a trifling third person,
a slave bound to diseased Time.
This body—unspoken,
meaningless, lifeless, drained—
a husk adrift
in the echo of her call.

How shall I go, O Queen—
break through this penetrated prison,
these walls of Meghnada, these iron doors?

I stand helpless—

a dead poet without refuge,
stranded in the famine of words,
where even language
has forgotten how to breathe.

Beating the drum of words,
he builds a palace of love—
For the empire of language,
he dares, again and again,
to cross the forbidden lines
he himself once drew.

The Word itself is a magician—
and Wordless, the God.
Witness to the crucified emperor,
Mahākāla—
this timeless time—
stands still,
listening.

Love

That tall, dark man—
he never knew
that with a single letter,
this Mahabharata would become impure.

In blind faith, he gathered everything—
and in a single, shattering moment,
the hand of connection
broke away.

He does not fear effort;
his faith is entirely his own.
Love is the fruit of a rare kingdom—
how could this dark man
ever understand it?
In camp heart-wrenching toil—
my dearest heartbeat!
How do you endure the days,
in the constant absence
of my garden,
bereft of its joy?

With each passing year, each fleeting season,
will love survive, or will it die?
In the long wait for this answer,
the days slip quietly by.

My Beloved

A fistful of smoke—this life,
only today,
tomorrow vanishes.
So much pride, yet for nothing.

Spilling like milk—
oh, what a fragile, helpless state,
my beloved!

In a kingdom without words,
how many suffer?
A miserable state—
from birth to death,
smokeless smoke,
all contained in a fistful of smoke,
uncountable fires burning within.

In the fire-red Holi of blood,
the fire throng surges—
from first light to fading dusk,
a towering mountain of smoke
envelops all,
swallowing sky and earth alike.

How much flesh, how much bitterness in this life!
Caught in the net of smoke,

trembling like fish,
swaying on the swing of fate—
this sorrowful mind hangs,
suspended in silent despair.

From dawn to dusk,
smokeless smoke,
life itself a smoke.
Burning within a fistful of smoke,
it becomes
a silent garden of peace.

Devi

On your forehead, kumkum of strange, radiant hue,
day by day it gleams,
a white glyph of light.

Truly, you are a goddess,
arriving on your own,
bestowing upon this earth
the blessing of a sacred, auspicious presence.

In sun, rain, cold, and mist,
your touch—soft, tender—
wrapped in the withered garland
of a shriveled hibiscus.
A piercing chill fills
this fierce, sorrowful heart.

In the tender bond of filial love,
your love—bound to me—
with eyes like green lotuses,
filled with the warmth of the rising sun.

Through wondrous will, the Trikal moves,
you, the all-desiring one,
and at the sway of your wish,
the very earth shivers
beneath your silent command.

O divine beauty!
Your adornment, strange and radiant,
each hue and shade
a subtle veil of transcendence,
shimmering like the hidden light of the cosmos.

When you open your lips,
the fragrance of sandalwood
when you close them again,
it blooms anew—
a thousand blue lotuses
scattering their scent across the night.

From the mantra of a single pious soul,
my very nerves tremble.
From your navel flows the river Ganga,
a living symbol of love and compassion.

O Mother!
Embrace me once,
fold me in the boundless warmth
of your love.

Enraptured by Her Love

The woman I fell in love with
appears before me, like a goddess
Flickers like a distant star
in the vast blue sky,
floating upon clouds
woven with sorrow and contemplation.
Then, with a stubborn grace,
she drifts away,
leaving only the whisper
of her fleeting light.

In one stubborn resolve,
she crossed three lines,
and dynasties trembled at her fire.
In another stubborn resolve,
she left the husband's son,
and let herself be drenched
in the sacred flood of love.
In yet another stubborn resolve,
her hair was washed
in the crimson ocean of blood,
each strand a song of sorrow and flame.

And in one unyielding, steadfast will,
around her neck a garland of scorn,

yet in my embrace she hangs—
forever bound,
unyielding, luminous, eternal.

I have fallen in love with a woman—
her face, pale as moonlight,
her eyes, twin sapphires in a boundless sky.
Slender wrists, hair like rivers unbound,
breasts sculpted sharp against the air,
her gaze—imprinted, unerasable.
At her soft, honeyed touch,
every limb quivers,
my nerves ignite in silent shivers.
The poet stands helpless,
lost in the symphony of her presence,
this fragile, trembling life
spinning in a thousand awe-struck gestures,
each one a hymn of longing,
fear, and rapture.

In this miserable life, the poet dreams—
alone, alone,
her face appears before him,
a goddess risen in delicate light.

In a basket of blossoms,
her hair adorned with flowers,
all sorrow wiped away,
nestled in her veil.
The poet reaches to touch her,
but his hands cannot grasp her.
Like a withered hibiscus,

she smiles—
radiant, teasing, untouchable,
yet ever beyond his reach.

I have fallen in love with a woman,
and her shadow looms, a trembling fear,
pressing upon me,
tossing me down again and again.
By some wondrous, stubborn will,
her form slips through my grasp,
no word escapes her parted lips,
and the living are undone by countless mishaps.
Beside the still river,
my body and soul drift
like a solitary boatman,
adrift on waters endless and silent,
reaching for her,
yet never touching her light.

Like a goddess, you appear—
your face resting in a basket of flowers,
adorning your hair with blooms,
forgetting, for a while, your own sorrow.
I reach out to touch you,
my trembling hand extended,
yet you slip away—
like an unseen bird,
rising, soaring, vanishing into air.
My grief remains unspent,
echoing through the hollows of my heart,
where your fragrance lingers,
but your form is gone.

The wondrous season of sorrow—
falling in love clouds the mind,
and in the intoxication of desire,
all sin and virtue
fade into oblivion.

No path lies before me,
and before I know it, the day fades away.
In the raging currents of endless rivers,
sorrow alone is my only companion.

I am in love with a woman—
she lives in every breath I take,
flickering like a distant star
against the vast blue sky.

Black Eagle Books

www.blackeaglebooks.org
info@blackeaglebooks.org

Black Eagle Books, an independent publisher, was founded as a nonprofit organization in April, 2019. It is our mission to connect and engage the Indian diaspora and the world at large with the best of works of world literature published on a collaborative platform, with special emphasis on foregrounding Contemporary Classics and New Writing.

www.ingramcontent.com/pod-product-compliance
Lightning Source LLC
Chambersburg PA
CBHW060559080526
44585CB00013B/626